Dear Jazmin,
I hope you en
to adulthood with me!
Thank you & Be well!

BLACK WOMAN GROWN

A CHILDish Continuation

KL

BY

KishaLynn Moore Elliott

This book reflects the author's present recollection of experiences over time. Portions of these stories have been fictionalized. Event timelines have been compressed, and dialogue has been recreated. Names and identifying details have been changed to protect the privacy of individuals and institutions.

This Stuff's Working! Publishing

ISBN: 978-1-7340963-4-7

DEDICATION

This book is dedicated to the first Black woman
I ever loved—my mother, Monica Ellen Billups.

Even though we stumbled and fell many times,
we rose and healed many more.

We grew together.

You taught me how to be an independent,
intelligent, unstoppable Black woman.

Thank you for the sacrifices you made as a mother.

Grace to the mistakes we both made.

Love and honor to you always.

ACKNOWLEDGEMENTS

My sincere gratitude…

To my forever Lord and Savior, Jesus Christ, through Whom all things have been proven possible for me time and again. Thank you for every footprint in the sand.

To my wife and love for life, Shelli Elliott. Thank you for standing by all my sides on this journey of being married, being mothers, and being magical-ass bitches. I will always love you more tomorrow.

To my son, Simeon, who is old enough to read and smart enough to write his own books. I love you. I'm proud of you. Thanks for sharing space with Mommy's fiftyleven jobs. I do it all for you and the child(ren) you may have one day.

To my mentor, my editor, my archivist, my friend, my mirror, and my muse: Sanda Balaban. No count of words could fully express my gratitude to you. I promise to keep trying to do so verbally and in writing for the rest of our long lives together.

To my Black Woman Grown Publishing Team: Leslie Schwartz—Editor (https://leslieschwartz.com); Otim Oloya—Cover Design (http://www.oloyadesign.com); Bill Weiss—Website Design (https://www.spintheweb.com); Abdul Rehman—Formatting (https://www.fiverr.com/abdulrehman17); Ghia Larkins—Front Cover Photo (https://ghialarkins.com); Jazzmine Taylor—Author Photos (https://www.jazzminemariephotography.com.)

A very special thanks to these institutions who helped make my DREAM of college come true:

Dorchester High School and the Academy of Public Service
Urban Scholars Program at UMASS-Boston
Summer Search Foundation
The Medill School of Journalism at Northwestern University
Trefler Foundation
Spelman College
Occidental College

I want to thank this BY-NO-MEANS EXHAUSTIVE list of the framily members who were crucial parts of my creative process and superfans who cheered me on over the last five years to get this next batch of stories down and out: Afira DeVries, CaMesha LaMon Reece, Carla Warnock, Chantel Quarles, Connie Self, Crystal Harris, Cynthia McGee-Burton, Eboni Harvey, Jerome Scott, Jesse Leon, Jessica Reed, Judy and Val Koss, Kandi Cole, Katherine Calihan Kennedy, Kelli Elliott, Kendrick Dial, Keomi Tarver, Kristi Hines Baker, Lauren Marie Fleming, Linda Moore, Mandi Jo, Marisol Alvarado, Mary Sotelo, Miki Vale and SOULKISS Theater, Nurith Amatai-Crawford, Phylissia Ricard Clark, Rachelle Archer, Ron Stallworth, Jr., Ronise Zenon, Sarah Steele, Seth James Ellis, Shae Fuller, and Shatrice Williams. Most importantly…my deepest gratitude and love to YOU, my dear reader:

____

(Write Your Name Here)

Finally, peace, gratitude, and light to those who will remain unnamed but will always be remembered.

Sincerely,

KishaLynn Moore Elliott

TABLE OF CONTENTS

CONTENT WARNING: Stories in this book depict explicit sexual content, self-harm, racism, homophobia, domestic violence, police brutality, and references to the 9/11 terrorist attack on the United States. Please practice discretion and prioritize self-care as you read.

PROLOGUE: 5.0

Before I even knew what college was, I wanted to go.

I was ten years old, living in Tampa, Florida with my mother and stepfather when Vanilla Ice released his hit single, *"Ice, Ice, Baby."* The song had a slick, colorful music video that featured Vanilla Ice dancing and rapping in the shadows wearing baggy clothes. I was obsessed with the video from the moment I first saw it on MTV. I taped it on the VCR and rewound it over and over, memorizing the lyrics and practicing the hip-hop choreography.

My favorite part of the video came in the middle of the song's second verse. Vanilla Ice cruised across my TV screen driving a glistening white Ford Mustang convertible 5.0, dropping its top in perfect rhythm with the song. That convertible was my dream car. I could practically feel the wind in my hair as I closed my eyes and imagined myself riding in slow motion down the street in my own 5.0 one day. I was inspired to share this vision with my Mom.

"Hey Mom. Guess what?" I asked her one day while she stood at the stove in the kitchen cooking spaghetti.

"What?" She pulled the spaghetti pot off the stove and moved it to the sink to drain off the water in a colander.

"One day, I'm gonna have a 5.0," I said.

My Mom looked at me, unamazed. "That's gonna be really hard Kisha. It takes all As on your report card. Even with that, I think the highest GPA you can get is a 4.0." She emptied the colander back into the pot, and begin mixing in her meat sauce.

I was confused. What did my report card have to do with driving a car? And what was a GPA? Before I could ask, she continued.

"But, with a GPA that good, I'll bet you can get a scholarship to college. And you're going to need one, because I won't be able to pay for it."

College. It was a word I had read about in books and heard occasionally at school, but I wasn't fully sure what it was. I just knew it was a place that people left to go to. For that reason alone, it interested me.

"Mom, a 5.0 is a car. A convertible," I said.

"Oh, well, I'll tell you what. If you get a full scholarship to college, then I will buy you a brand new car when you graduate from high school."

The goal of college and the promise of earning that car from my mother held fast in my heart throughout the rest of my secondary education. These were the toughest years of my childhood as I weathered one sad day after the next in isolation and overcame one trauma after another at home and at school.

By the time I reached my senior year in high school, I had the 4.0 GPA, but we weren't stable. We had moved from one home to the next, ultimately being evicted from our home and forced to cohabitate in a dilapidated home with my mother's friend Audrey.

A part of me always knew there would be no car for me at graduation. But there would be college. By any means necessary. I had Vanilla Ice and my Mom to thank for it.

###

BLACK CHERUB

I arrived at The University in Evanston, Illinois the summer of 1997 an absolute wreck. I was participating in a program that called us "Cherubs." The program promised self-discovery for rising high school seniors through the exploration of a career in journalism. I was already a writer and aspiring author, so I was eager to explore a new professional pathway. I attended on a scholarship I received from an organization that sent at-risk youth on life-changing summer experiences.

An African-American student advisor was the first to greet me. She gave me two keys and a room assignment. A young, Italian instructor next helped me lug my bags up the three flights of stairs. I took a deep labored breath at the end of the hallway, mentally preparing myself to confront my first ever roommate. I wondered if she had arrived yet.

Not many people had arrived yet, just enough to make me feel instantly weird—they were all white. I stood in front of my assigned room door and with another deep breath, swung the door open. I stood shocked for a brief moment as my brain caught up to what my eyes were seeing—one bed, one desk, one closet. In fact, there had only been one name on the door—mine. I had been assigned to a single. Exhaling, I had the insane desire to laugh and cry at the same time. I was both disappointed and elated. Still bewildered, I yanked my things into my room and shut the door. My door. To my room.

Being an only child, I was no stranger to having a room to myself, but somehow here it did not seem natural. It was like I had been told of a visitor's arrival, had both anticipated and prepared for that arrival, only to find that there was no visitor at all, or that I myself was the visitor.

I started to unpack my things. I hung my favorite poster-a black and white print of a lonely Labrador dog staring wistfully out of a rain-splattered window with his paw against the glass. I dressed my bed with my over-sized sheets from home, having not been able to afford the correct twin sized sheets. I plugged in my radio cassette player and lamented the fact that my CD's would be of no use, as I had hoped my roommate might have a CD player.

I began to wonder how many others had received single rooms. I sought the answer in the orientation packet. After wading through a weekly schedule and a blurb about the program, I located the program statistics. We were 88 students, from all over the United States. There were six single rooms in the dorm, one right next door to me.

"Next door," I thought. "I have neighbors."

I glanced at my closed door and realized the "leave-me-alone" impression that it might be giving off. I walked over and swung it open too eagerly. More people had begun to arrive. I peeked out, then decided to walk down the hallway, survey the group, and see if I could make some instant friends, or at least make myself known.

I walked by many open doors and said hello when someone noticed me. Parents bustled about helping unpack while their daughters had already begun to bond with each other. I felt self-conscious about being there by myself, as my mother had not come with me. As I watched TVs, computers, and stereos assembled, I became keenly aware of some class differences. All of these revelations were crammed under one final realization—I was the only Black person. I wondered if that was why I had a single room.

I suddenly felt like a target for fake smiles that projected "hello" but really meant, "Oh, there's a Black girl on this floor." I surrendered to the urge to retreat and went back to my lonely room, not knowing what to do next. I pondered leaving my door open to allow for potential socializing, but then shut it with a resounding slam.

"I can do this." I said out loud to myself.

"This was a mistake," my brain replied.

I was stunned by the lack of racial diversity in the program. I had never been *such* the minority, especially coming from Boston, where there were all types of Black people everywhere. In addition, my poorness was a major concern for me. Based on what I saw other students moving into their rooms, it was clear that these students were not attending on scholarships. I did not feel I could relate to anyone there, and having a single room really capped off how I was feeling and would feel for the rest of the summer—isolated and lonely.

I believe all things happen for a reason, good and bad. One of my favorite biblical scriptures says: *"Consider it pure joy, my brothers, whenever you face trials of many kinds; because you know that the testing of your faith develops perseverance. Perseverance must finish its work so that you may be mature and complete, not lacking in anything."* **James 1:2-4**

So, I tried to be optimistic. I threw myself into the workload of the program, which was very intensive.

I kept a journal for the first few days of the program. On July 1, 1997, day three at The University, I wrote:

"My worst fear has come to life. I am feeling...alone. I really don't have anything in common with anyone. Most of them are white, which is not a problem to me, but I am beginning to wonder whether my "Blackness" makes them feel uncomfortable around me. Yes, people are nice, but despite my efforts, no one is really eager to bond with me."

These problems plagued me the entire summer. I was unable to relate to anyone, even the Black students that were there. I was not actually the only Black student. There were four Black Cherubs total, and one Black student advisor. The Black student advisor treated me like I was an inferior, and I did not feel comfortable around her. One of the Black students was a male who told me he would rather hang out with the white people than with "us" (the other three Black girls there), then ignored us for the rest of the summer.

Another Black girl continually rejected my efforts to get to know her, and she rarely came out of her room—she also had a single, which deepened my suspicion that our room assignments were racially motivated. Intimidation kept me from getting to know the last Black student; she looked mean, and I was afraid to approach her. Plus, she was the one of us who had a roommate. They were close, so I felt she didn't need a friend the way I did.

I tried to make friends with some of the white students there, but none of them acted comfortable around me, and after the first week, most had split off into cliques. On the Fourth of July of that year, I watched the fireworks alone, and absolutely no one spoke to me, even though I attempted to start conversations. Devastated, I gave up altogether.

I completely isolated myself—I spent all of my free time in the college's Computer Room, trolling for online companionship. My typical day was to wake up, attend the day's lessons and complete my assignments, eat a lonely meal in the cafeteria, then lock myself in the computer lab until curfew, when I would check in at the dorm and go to bed.

Some nights, I cried myself to sleep, but most nights I just found myself angry—angry with myself for not succeeding in my journalism classes and angry with my peers for rejecting me. During weeks two and three, I was at the height of misery, and hated myself more each day.

One evening, I returned to my room to find the racist message, "Blacks are disgusting," written on my dry-erase board. I erased it and say nothing. For the first time in my life, I felt like my race was a problem. I started to hate myself for being the minority, even though it was not my fault. I was stunned at these feelings; this was not the type of self-discovery I was expecting from this program.

One night, when I just could not stand to be in my room alone any longer, I went downstairs and sat in the lobby, in tears. For hours, people walked by me and ignored me. I drew a sketch while sitting there. In this sketch, I portrayed the negative emotions I was feeling. "Pissed," "Hate," "Broken-hearted," and "I Hate Me," all appeared amidst the angry drawing which scared me then and still does now.

I longed to leave the program, but I still had two weeks to go. All I really could do was pray for endurance, and I did. In the middle of the fourth week, just a few nights after my lobby breakdown, there was a knock on my door. I opened it to find the mean-looking Black girl, Tiara, standing there. She introduced herself and asked if she could see how I had decorated my room. I was so happy to have a guest that I almost cried. That night, she and I became friends. We spent nights in the last two weeks of the program talking, often until sunrise. I was finally able to share with someone how I had been feeling throughout the summer. I regretted not having had the courage to approach her sooner. She told me she'd been feeling the same way.

In spite of my late-blooming friendship with Tiara, I counted the days until I would leave The University. When the program concluded, I was relieved to be leaving. I felt cheated and I felt like I had wasted my time. I did not attend the closing ceremony for the Cherub Program. I had no need to say goodbye to anyone. While 87 Journalism Cherubs gathered to celebrate and reminisce over the past five weeks of that summer, I quickly and silently packed up my room and called a cab, leaving the dorm as alone and unnoticed as I was when I arrived. I carried with me the realization that college may not turn out to be the dream life I imagined. However, it still beat the harsh realities of life at home.

Returning to Boston was no picnic. I arrived to a home that was even more squalid than before because the living room ceiling had collapsed. Then, not even six hours after I got home, my mother woke me to tell me that my grandfather was dead. I was devastated, still tender from the loss of my grandmother a few months prior.

My summer was officially enveloped by the loss of two people who were very important to me. My grandmother's death had been a sudden tragedy to me; I did not even know she was ill. I later learned that she had insisted on my ignorance of her deteriorating condition. The day after I got home from Illinois, I was back on a plane to Ohio to see my favorite grandfather be buried next to my grandfather. While I was gone, my mother moved us into a new house.

It seemed to me that the entire summer was a failure. In all I had expected to gain, I felt I had totally lost. I was bitter and disappointed and stayed that way well into the first quarter of my senior year. Still motivated, I focused on college applications, applying to nine schools, mostly in Chicago and Ohio. Since I knew it was up to me to pay for college, I also completed every scholarship application I could get my hands on.

Then, one Friday in January, just as a light snow had begun, I rounded the corner of our street walking home from school and saw a bunch of our stuff sitting out on the sidewalk. I broke into a run towards the house, believing we were being robbed. I stopped short when I saw my mother exiting the front door with a box in her hands.. Her face was ashen, her eyes were swollen from tears. She didn't even look at me. "We're being evicted."

I had no clear idea why we were being evicted—we had just moved in—or where we were going to go, or what we were going to do. Suddenly we were homeless.

My Mom found a space for us to stay with a friend of hers who lived right behind the house we were kicked out of. The friend, Audrey, was living on an undisclosed disability, so she didn't work. She was a pottery artist, a self-professed weed addict, and a hoarder. We were grateful that she opened her home to us. She even helped us walk our stuff over. However, the house itself was on the verge of being condemned. Filth accumulated everywhere. Every inch of it was filthy and crammed with items that seemed useless and dangerous. Stacks of newspaper. A piano with only six keys on it. Years' worth of mail piled high on a shelf behind the door. Even the walls and ceiling were dirty.

I took a shower and felt dirtier stepping out of it than I did getting in. It was a nightmare. But it was better than a winter night on the freezing streets of Boston. So I repressed my disgust and swallowed my complaints. Whenever I was tempted to wonder why life offered me nothing but challenges, I would remind myself that I was no angel, and barely a Cherub.

###

GUIDANCE COUNSELING

I initially applied to eight colleges. My top choices were all in the Midwest, but my heart was set on attending school in Chicago. I had a 4.0 GPA coming into my senior year, and a 3.8 GPA overall. I felt pretty confident as I meticulously typed my applications on a typewriter in my high school's brand-new computer lab.

I worked alone on my college applications. Truth be told, I had no clue what I was doing. Neither my mother nor father had gone to college. My teachers were encouraging, but I didn't have the courage to ask them to walk me through the process. My overworked guidance counselor was useless.

"It's up to you to complete your applications on time. I can't help you with anything more than a fee waiver, an envelope and a stamp," She said, a dismissal outright.

So, I used the best resource I had at hand—the application forms. I studied them carefully and set about following them carefully and thoroughly. Each application required something different—it was exhausting and confusing to manage across nine colleges. But I pushed through, typing my information carefully onto small lines on that typewriter. The clack of the keys stroking the pages would have been hypnotic if I wasn't so concerned about not making a mistake.

Soon I completed all the college applications and gathered all the materials required to submit them—my transcript, my high school resume of extracurriculars and accomplishments, short essay responses, several signed letters of recommendation, and most importantly, my personal statement.

I wrote my personal statement about the time I spent in foster care in fourth grade. The essay focused on the relationship I built with my oldest foster sibling, who was deaf. I talked about why I learned American Sign Language to communicate with her and for her. I was very proud of the essay. The only problem with the essay was its length—18 pages when I finished my first draft. The limit was five pages. I was stuck. Fortunately, I was in a college preparatory program at a local college and was able to go to my favorite instructor, Perkins, for help shrinking my personal statement down into a powerful five pages.

"You're going to get into any college that reads this," Perkins said when we finished.

"Let's hope so. And that I can afford to go if I do," I replied.

"Are you applying for many scholarships? With your writing skills, I bet you could get a ton of financial support for college."

"I'm applying for those next. Just had to get these applications out of the way. It's been hard."

"I can imagine. Well, I have two pieces of advice, if I may?"

"Sure."

"First, apply for any and every scholarship you can get your hands on. Show them this essay. You can do it. You're a rockstar."

"Okay, I will. And the second piece?"

"Well, it's less advice and more of a threat?"

"A threat? Okay..."

"You better keep up this writing, or you're gonna be in big trouble with me."

I laughed.

"Okay, I'll apply for *all* the scholarships. And I'll keep writing. Thank you for your help."

The next day, I proudly huffed into Ms. Willis, my guidance counselor's, office the minute the school day ended, my backpack heavy with the weight of eight completed college applications.

"Are you kidding me? How many colleges are you applying for?" She seemed pissed.

"Eight."

"Well damn why don't you just take all the fee waivers?"

"I'm sorry. I didn't know there was a limit." I began to feel scared. The application fees ranged from $25-$75 each. I couldn't afford to pay them without the waivers.

"Well, not many of our seniors apply to four-year colleges, so I guess it's fine to give you a few extra.

Ms. Willis reached over her cluttered desk into a file holder and grabbed a stack of small forms. She handed them to me.

"You'll need to fill one of these out for each application. And hurry up. I'm already supposed to be gone, but I know there's deadlines and things. I'll give you a few minutes so they can go out in the mail tomorrow."

I sat outside her office and frantically scribbled my information on the eight application fee waiver forms.

When I returned to her, she handed me eight letter sized envelopes. "Address these to the colleges."

With a sigh I left her office again, and painstakingly copied the addresses from each application onto the envelopes.

Back in her office again, she frowned impatiently as I presented my work. "Okay, let's do this one at a time. Hand me the first application."

I handed over my top choice first. She stapled it together with the fee waiver on top, then folded the thick packet of paper into thirds. Finally, she stuffed it all into the envelope. It was so thick that she had to tape it closed. Then, I watched in horror as she placed exactly one first class stamp in the upper right-hand corner.

"Don't you think it will need more postage than that?" I asked.

"One stamp. That's all you get. You got the extra fee waivers. Don't get greedy," Ms. Willis snapped.

I remained silent as we repeated this process with the remaining seven applications. Some envelopes bulged more than others. All of them were taped shut. And they all had that one, insufficient stamp on board to carry my dreams to Chicago and Ohio.

Ms. Willis walked past me and placed the chunky envelopes haphazardly into the outgoing mail slot outside her office door.

"There. Nice work," she said to herself.

That made me feel angry—it *was my* nice work. She had barely helped at all. And now I worried that my hard work would even reach their destinations on time because of the postage. I seethed inside but remained calm—I wasn't about to go toe-to-toe with Ms. Willis. I still needed her.

She looked surprised when she turned around and saw I was still standing there.

"Why are you still here?" she asked, looking down at me.

"I need scholarships. To help pay for college."

"Well, no kidding kid. I saw the places you applied to. Them fancy Chicago colleges ain't cheap. If you even get in. Ha."

That broke me. Tears welled up in my eyes. She must have seen my chin trembling because she sighed and softened her voice.

"Go on look in the second drawer of that file cabinet. There's a folder that says "Scholarships" somewhere in there. Anytime I get one, I stick it in there. Just take whatever applications you can find. No one else ever asks about stuff like that."

I pulled the file drawer open and found the scholarship file, crammed with paper application forms for various scholarships. I remembered my UMB instructor's advice and I decided to take them all. I lifted the entire file out of the file drawer. That's when I saw it—right behind the "Scholarships" file was a folder labeled

"The College." I recognized the name immediately, but it took me a while to firmly place it.

"Hey, isn't that that college on the Cosby Show?" I asked my counselor.

"Hurry up I don't have all night. It's supposed to snow and I'm still here wasting time with you."

Without another thought, I snatched The College's file from the drawer as well, put them both in my backpack and left her office.

"Thanks," I muttered. As I passed through the office and out into the school hallway, I added, "You miserable bitch."

That night in my bedroom I sorted through all the scholarship applications. Some were recent but most were from previous years. I could tell which ones were annual because there were multiple applications across the years. The amounts ranged from $250 to $10,000. The larger scholarships were renewable; the smaller ones were one-time funds. I decided to apply for every one. Most of them wanted the same information I had submitted with my college applications. All of them would accept my personal statement and letters of recommendation.

Oh yeah, this is happening.

Next my eyes glanced at The College file. I opened it and saw there was a brochure, and the paper application form. The form was dated for the Fall 2015 admission—three years old. I thumbed through the brochure and saw vibrant photos of Black women with straightened hair, wearing smiles and light blue t-shirts. For a moment, I could see myself among them. I learned from reading the brochure that The College was a Historically Black College for women. My high school was predominantly Black, and I had been around Black folks most of my life. I wanted to experience something different in college, so Historically Black Colleges and Universities, or HBCU's, didn't naturally appeal to me.

However, the idea of a women's college was attractive. Especially once I learned that a historically Black college for men was right across the street. The brochure said that The College was in Atlanta, Georgia. I didn't even know where Georgia was on the map—and here I was a senior in high school. The thought made me laugh.

I looked for the list of majors and was disappointed that there were only a handful. The College is a Liberal Arts college, not a large university like the schools I preferred. However, they did offer a major in Psychology. I was determined to become a sex therapist one day, so I was already declaring Psychology as my intended major.

Finally, I reached the end of the brochure. The names of various The College alumna were listed:

Alice Walker

Esther Rolle

And Keshia Knight Pulliam, whom I had idolized in her role as Rudy in the Cosby Show. She was a current student at that time.

Suddenly I was putting pen to that paper application. Screw the typewriter. This was just an experiment. I completed the application quickly, then made sure it didn't require any extra materials that weren't in my college application packet. It didn't. I even had a fee waiver left from the stack my counselor had handed over.

The next morning, I was back at my counselors with my The College application already stuffed and sealed.

"I just need one more stamp," I begged her, showing her the envelope.

"The College huh?" I noticed she was almost smiling. That was different.

"Did you put a fee waiver in there?

"Yes, I had an extra one. And a transcript. Everything's in there."

"Okay, I'll mail it." She went to her desk and retrieved a stamp. No luck on any extra postage, not even for The College.

My counselor dropped the application in the slot.

"Thank you," I said, turning to leave.

"Wait," she called. She handed me a stack of envelopes. "Bring me your scholarship applications in these envelopes. I'll insert your transcripts and mail them for you."

It was one of the kindest things this woman had ever done for me.

Over the next two months, I returned to her office daily with a newly completed scholarship application. She processed and mailed them all without complaint, but also without compliment. She barely even glanced at them. I was just grateful that she was cooperating. At that stage, I didn't need anything more from her than the bare minimum guidance counseling she had given. It was enough.

###

TEARS IN MY POLENTA

Every time I feel figuratively dead or dying inside, I seek inspiration.

When a dream feels like it is dying, I find inspiration.

When a goal feels unachievable, I turn to my sources of inspiration.

Inspiration is all around me as sure as life is happening all around me. So, I often don't have to look far or long to get back on track.

But in the darkest days, or for the most distant desires, I have a sure, inedible, and infinite source of inspiration. My muse, my mirror, my Mira.

Mira is my mentor. She was assigned to me decades ago when I was still in high school through a mentorship program, but our relationship quickly superseded its extracurricular origin.

Mira wasn't my first mentor. She was my second; the first mentor I was assigned abandoned me after just one month of the six-month commitment. No explanation, no goodbye, just ghosted. When I met her, she was engaged to a coworker. I shadowed her at work once and met him. On the surface they looked different, but I didn't know either of them well enough to judge their compatibility. Shortly after the job shadow my mentor told me she had called off her engagement. That was the last time I ever heard from her.

When that match died, it took with it my best hope for guidance navigating the process of college applications. As the only child of a single teenage Mom, I was bound to be first generation college student. I had everything it took—I knew I did. Great grades. Tons of extracurriculars and community service, a bomb ass personal statement essay on my experience as a foster youth, intelligence, humor, and amazing writing skills. I just needed someone to take my hand and put it all my attributes together. But my mentor ditched me.

Enter Mira. She didn't float in from the sky on an umbrella like Mary Poppins or anything. No, I actually had to press the issue. I was terrified about financial aid, college selection process, so many things I would need to do right. I was in a homeless situation at the time and getting to college felt very much like life and death for me.

I was persistent and requested another mentor. The program leader said she had a friend who refused to be a mentor, but she felt we were meant to be. She matched me to Mira, and she was right.

Mira gave me life from the moment I first met her. She was late to our first mentor event. I was losing hope, until she exploded into the room holding root beer in her hands and apologies for her tardiness spilling from her lips. I accepted them both. Then, we turned to each other and started a conversation that has literally never stopped for 22 years. I mean, we've had to press pause of course to sleep and eat and like, live life, but the conversation just keeps going because it gives so much life.

Mira and I were in sync from the start, even though we weren't the same race, age, or religion. For a person who says she refused to be a mentor, Mira showed up to it with a very full heart. We dove in together and swam deep. She had fascinating answers to my questions—even the ones not related to college. She made me see myself and the world differently. She was the perfect sage to help season my dreams for the future. It seemed our conversations only began; they never ended.

Mira also entered my life at the perfect time. We hit the ground running together toward my goal to escape to college. With acceptance letters in hand to all nine colleges I had applied to, funding was at the top of my mind. I was still waiting for those colleges to send me my financial aid offers and waiting to find out how many of the external scholarships I applied for would be awarded to me. I shared my worries with Mira, who constantly reassured me that the money would be there. I believed it. I had done my best.

I hated being at home because our living situation was so miserable. Fortunately, I was involved in many extracurricular activities and trusted as a leader at my school, so I often remained on campus for hours after the school day ended. My teachers allowed me to use the computer lab as much as I wanted to work on my scholarship search. One late afternoon, I left the computer lab to head home when I bumped into a white woman I didn't know in the hallway.

"Oh, hello!" she greeted me. "The school day ended a while ago. What are you still doing here?"

Even though this woman was a stranger, I decided to answer her honestly.

"I've been in the computer lab, trying to figure out how to pay for college," I said.

"No kidding?" she replied. "Hey, I think I know who you are—is your name KishaLynn?"

I looked at her in surprise; I had never seen her before. How did she know my name?

"Yes, that's me," I answered.

"Hi, KishaLynn. My name is Patricia. I used to be a student teacher here, another lifetime ago," she chuckled a little. I stared at her, still curious about who she was and how she knew me.

"So, how is the path to college going?" she asked.

"Well, it's going great if I let the acceptance letters tell it. I got into every college I applied to," I said.

"That's fantastic!" she said. "Congratulations."

"Thank you," I replied. "My challenge now is finding money. It's…a struggle," I said. My voice faded a little as I thought about our living situation. I didn't want to overshare with a stranger about my mother or our living situation.

"Well, paying for college shouldn't be an obstacle for a student like you," she said. "I'll tell you what. When you decide what school you're going to, let me know. I want to help you get where you're going. Your teachers have told me about you, and I want to assist you. I'm around doing some work to support the school. Your teachers know how to contact me."

I looked her up and down curiously. I thought she was joking—or crazy. Either way, I didn't believe her. I didn't even know her.

"Umm, sure. OK, thanks. I have to get going. I'll see you around," I said.

"Yes, you will. Take care, KishaLynn." She gave a cheerful wave and continued down the hallway as I headed out the door.

That night I called Mira and relayed the strange encounter to her.

"Wow! That sounds amazing!" Mira exclaimed.

"Yeah, but she can't be serious. What does she mean—help me get where I'm going?"

"It sounds like a scholarship opportunity. And it could be a big one—do you know who you met?" Mira asked.

"Nope. Not a clue," I answered.

"She's a philanthropist."

"What is a philanthropist?" I asked.

"A philanthropist is a person who donates money," Mira answered.

I sat up in my bed and leaned into the phone.

"Mira, are you saying she's rich?"

"I would say so. She runs a local foundation that issues grants to several worthy causes. I can't think of a cause more worthy than your education. I think you should take her seriously. It sounds like she believes in you—or many people believe in you since your reputation preceded your meeting."

"It can't be real," I said. "No one just walks up to you randomly and offers to pay for your college education."

"Well, Patricia isn't just anybody. And neither are you, KishaLynn."

"So, how do I find out if she is serious?" I asked.

"Would you like me to reach out and get more information?" Mira asked.

"You'd do that for me?"

"Without a doubt," Mira answered. "Let me contact your teachers tomorrow and see what I can learn. Then, I'll have an update at the mentor/mentee meeting tomorrow afternoon."

The moment Mira arrived at my school the following afternoon, she rushed up to me.

"She's serious!" Mira said. Her voice carried a high pitch of excitement. "Patricia is serious about paying for you to go to school. She's creating a scholarship fund, and, as I understand it, she's prepared to cover the entire expense of your college education."

I couldn't process the information. I was sure Mira was lying, but I saw pride bursting from her eyes, and I knew she'd never joke about something so important.

"A…full scholarship?" I said incredulously.

"Looks like it," Mira said. "Come on; the meeting is about to start."

I could barely focus on the meeting. With a dose of doubt, I could only wonder if I genuinely no longer had to worry about paying for college. I was eager to get home, for once, and share this news with my mother.

When I got home from school that night, I poked my head into my mother's bedroom on my way up to my room in the attic.

"Mom, you'll never believe what happened today."

"What?" she asked. "Another acceptance letter?"

"No," I said. "I've heard back from all my schools already. But this is even better...apparently, a woman named Patricia told my teachers and my mentor that she would pay to send me to college. So she's creating a full scholarship."

I delivered this news, expecting my Mom to express some of the joy or relief I was beginning to feel about the opportunity. But, she sat still and silent on her bed. When she finally spoke, her words were crushing.

"Why would anyone do that for you?" she asked.

It was a question that hurt me so much to hear that I didn't bother answering. My Mom hadn't been engaged in my college process; I couldn't blame her much, given that we had lost our home and lived in bleak circumstances. I was a first-generation college student. I hadn't expected much help. But it hurt not to feel her immediate support. I slowly backed away from my Mom's bedroom door and ascended the rickety stairs to my bedroom in the attic. As I fell asleep that night, I reminded myself that I hadn't believed the news either. That kind of thing didn't happen to people like us.

When I got to school the next day, the word was out about the scholarship. My teachers congratulated me, and I realized it was real. Patricia was creating the full scholarship to college that I have been dreaming of receiving since I was ten years old. So I shifted my focus to that and stopped worrying about my Mom's underwhelming reaction. I thanked Mira profusely for helping me put the pieces together, but she refused to accept credit.

"You owe gratitude only to yourself and to Patricia, who is using her resources both generously and, might I add, wisely by investing in you," she said.

Next came the question of what school to go to. I no longer had to base my decision on financial aid. Patricia was willing to use the scholarship to send me to the school of my choice, no matter the cost. That's when the pressure to accept admission to The College became real. The College was never my dream. My dream schools were all in Chicago, with Ohio schools as a backup. I had applied to The College as an afterthought. I never expected to be accepted, and when I was, I never thought I could afford to attend. I didn't even know where Atlanta, Georgia was. All I knew was that every time I mentioned The College, people who were familiar with it lit up with enthusiasm for me.

"I don't even know where Atlanta is," I shared with Mira over the phone. I felt conflicted by the decision and tortured by the pressure to explore an option I wasn't familiar with beyond pop culture references on TV.

"Well, why don't we explore it further by arranging for you to take a trip and visit the campus?" Mira suggested.

I laughed at the thought.

"I have to make this decision soon. I can't just go to Atlanta right now. I don't have the money for that."

"I'll pay for you to go down there," Mira offered. "This isn't a decision you should make uninformed. I'd be happy to help you."

It seemed very important to Mira that I consider The College. I knew she had gone to a women's college and had loved her experience. She had shared that people in her network were advising her that an HBCU like The College would be right up my alley. I agreed with Mira that there was only one way to find out, so I accepted her help. The College had a special event for admitted students, and the timing lined up perfectly for me to participate. Mira purchased my airline ticket, and a few weeks later, I walked through The College's gates for an overnight visit.

Everything at The College differed from other colleges I visited and toured. I had never seen so many Black women gathered in one place. Throughout the event, The College was selling me sisterhood and camaraderie in an undeniable way. As an only child, the idea of sisterhood was foreign, but I wanted connection and belonging. However, I didn't love the location. It was hot and muggy in Atlanta, even in April. It reminded me of the sweltering heat of childhood summers in Florida. Also, the campus dorms and facilities were old and not updated. I had seen dorms resembling luxury condominiums on New England and Midwest college tours. The College dorms didn't even have air conditioning. As a small liberal arts school, The College's academic offerings were also lacking compared to the large universities that were my top choices. But, I was planning to major in Psychology and minor in writing. Both were possible at The College. That night, there was a sleepover for the accepted students in the basement of one of the freshman dorms. The conversation was virtually unanimous among the group that everyone was planning to attend The College in the fall. I fell asleep feeling conflicted and woke up still analyzing the pros and cons as I packed my bags and caught a taxi to the airport for my flight home.

The College wasn't the college of my dreams. However, it was the best college I had gotten into. The College had emphasized its low acceptance rate of the incoming freshman class. Nevertheless, I knew it was an honor to be accepted. Mira had sent me to visit there for a reason, and I felt the reason was to discover that it was the right college for me.

Why not give it a try? I thought.

So when I got back from the trip, I accepted admission to The College and announced my decision to Mira, my teachers, and Patricia, my benefactor. Everyone was elated for me. I finally relaxed and realized that I had accomplished my goals, despite all the obstacles, including homelessness.

The rest of the school year was drawn to a close, and high school graduation was near. I accepted the scholarship award from

Patricia. She had named it the "I've Got A Dream Scholarship"; I was its first recipient. I was happy my mother came to the ceremony. It felt like a success for us both. Then, Mira wrapped me in a tight congratulatory hug after the scholarship ceremony, gushing with pride. She was such a good mentor. I began to mourn that the program that had matched us was almost over, so I assumed that our mentoring relationship would end too. I said as much to her later that night on the telephone.

"Well, you're going to be free for me soon," I said. ""

"Free from you?" she said.

"Yeah," I said.

"Whatever do you mean by that?"

"Well, there's only a couple of weeks left in the mentorship program," I began. "Once the program ends, you no longer have to help me."

"Help you?" she said. "Is that what I've been doing? Helping you?" "Yes, you've been helping me a lot. I needed it. It's why I asked for a mentor. I know you didn't want to be a mentor. I'm glad you changed your mind. But I don't expect you to go further once the program ends."

"What?" Mira sounded deeply offended. "Listen, KishaLynn. You're stuck with me, honey! We don't have to stop talking just because the program ends."

"You're willing to keep helping me?" I asked.

"I don't like that you keep saying it like that like you're a charity cause. I'm not only helping you. I'm getting a lot out of this too. This is a relationship. I'm learning from you, and you are learning from me. You're helping me in ways that you probably can't even see. I'm so glad that my friend talked me into being your mentor. If you would like to continue this relationship beyond the program, I would be happy to. But, as I said, you are stuck with me."

I smiled at the phone. "OK, Mira," I said. "Let's keep going."

And we did. We committed to continue the relationship for as long as it had value. I left to attend The College, Mira and I spoke by phone every month.

After my Fall semester, I returned to Boston from college in Atlanta for Christmas break. Mira and I had planned to meet up to do something artistically fabulous, which we are prone to do. That evening I believe she'd taken me to see some friends of hers perform a part of an improv comedy group in Cambridge Square. Afterwards, she took me to a very nice Italian restaurant for dinner.

After looking at the menu, I decided to order a polenta dish, which is cornmeal mash. When our food arrived, I took one bite of the creamy, savory goop and instantly fell in love with the flavor and the texture of polenta. Every taste of the dish was pure heaven. In the midst of my indulgence in a new-found ambrosia, Mira dropped the bomb that she was moving from Boston, back to New York.

The world paused. The deliciousness of that polenta evaporated as the news sank in. And next came tears. First a trickle, then a stream, followed by a *deluge* of tears. It was an impressive display of emotion. No one was more shocked than Mira herself. Why was I so upset by this news when I no longer lived in Boston myself?

To me, her departure represented a loss. I was (quite irrationally) fearful of the sudden end of our mentorship and friendship. I (quite wrongfully) attributed her location in Boston as the reason we remained a part of each other's lives. I was reassured knowing that I could see her anytime I came to Boston during school breaks. Mira had already made her indelible mark on my existence. Mira found me. She saved me. She helped push me across the finish line. Anything that further separated us seemed to threaten the core of who I was then and who I was becoming. Losing Mira, by any means, was to lose my inspiration.

I couldn't explain any of this to Mira in the moment. I could only cry. The dinner ended, and we parted ways. Shortly after, I returned to The College and Mira moved to New York. Of course, we remained connected. In fact, we've grown so much closer despite the increasing geographical distances that newly separated us. One way or another, she and I have managed to keep reuniting from coast to coast. I have never known anyone as special as Mira. She is not just a mentor, but a friend, a confidante, a muse. She's the main reason I believe deeply in mentorship, and in myself.

###

GREGORY

Gregory was a guy I met online in an Alamak chat room during my junior year in high school. I spent a lot of time in these chat rooms as a teenager and built connections there that extended to the telephone. Some of those connections were just for phone sex. Some were friendships. A couple were "relationships."

Gregory was one of those "relationships."

My chat name back then was "ChocKiss" and his was, I kid you not, "SexualChocolate."

Given that we both had chocolate in our names, we hit it off in the chat rooms and started instant messaging each other. After that we slowly built towards cybersex, at which I was very good. He was not very good at it. His spelling and grammar were horrible. And he typed slow. I, on the other hand, had learned to type very fast by chatting and cybersexing for hours every evening over the past year. It took a long time for Gregory to message me back when we were chatting and having cybersex. But he was a kind and sweet guy, funny even. So that's probably why I invited him to exchange numbers and move things over to the phone.

The first time I talked to Gregory I immediately understood why his chat grammar was so shitty. He had a very thick foreign accent—one I readily recognized from Boston's melting pot of Black culture as Jamaican. There are a ton of Jamaicans and Haitians in Boston. Gregory lived in New York.

Phone sex was better than cybersex with Gregory. I thought his accent was sexy, and he was very easy to please. He made girlish squeaky sounds when he came. I often teased him about it.

But ultimately what I noticed very quickly is that I enjoyed talking to Gregory most when we weren't having phone sex. He was a Virgo, like me, born on September 1. He was an accountant, 23 years old. We had a lot in common and he was a jokester. I don't remember many details of our conversations now, but I do remember how much I would laugh talking to him. Soon we were talking during the daytime as well as late evening. He would call me, paying for the long distance.

Gregory knew about my interest in women, which then I was describing as bisexuality but that was still online/by phone only.

I had already lost my virginity a few months before I met Gregory but I had long ended my "experiment" with that still unnamed boy by then. Bored by that physical reality of sex, I returned to the more vibrant sexual experiences available to me on the internet in my cyber-relationships and phone dalliances.

After a few months of our relationship, Gregory and I decided we wanted to meet in person. So he offered to drive from New York to Boston one weekend.

I told Gregory I was 18 years old—a lie I told everyone online. In truth, I'd just turned 16 and had entered my junior year in high school. I would need a good excuse to spend a night away from home with him.

Fortunately for me, there was a high school Fall dance coming up.

I asked a friend of mine named Kelsey if we could have a sleepover at her house after the dance. Since we'd had them before she agreed.

Then I told her that *actually* I was going to go to her house from the high school dance and tell Gregory to pick me up from her apartment, which I would say was my apartment. I would go spend

Friday night at a hotel with him, instead of at her house. Then I would come back to her house and spend Saturday night there and go home on Sunday. Kelsey was all in on this plan and agreed to cover for me.

I told my Mom I was going to the dance, then spending the weekend at Kelsey's house. She gave me permission to go.

Friday night of the dance came. The fall dance was very lame but I didn't care. All I cared about was the fact that Gregory was already on the road on his way down from New York.

Kelsey's boyfriend had a car so he dropped us off at her place after the dance. Then we hung out together in the park waiting for Gregory to pull up. I didn't want to go into Kelsey's house because I didn't want her Mom to question why I was leaving so late. Kelsey was more excited than I was to see what was going to happen when I met Gregory. I felt some angst, but was not as nervous as I expected. Gregory and I knew each other well. There wasn't much we hadn't discussed or shared with each other in the months we had been chatting online and talking on the phone.

I'd told Gregory that I'd meet him outside. When he pulled up to the parking lot of Kelsey's apartment complex he was driving a black Mitsubishi Eclipse sports car. I climbed in and waved goodbye to Kelsey.

"That's my very worried best friend," I said, greeting him with a threatening glare. "She's writing down your license plate number in case anything bad happens to me."

"Well," he answered dryly. "There go my plans to rape and kill you." Then he cracked a smile which made me laugh.

"Hi," I said elbowing his arm as I pulled on my seatbelt and snapped it into place. "I'm Lynn. It's nice to finally meet you."

I looked at him and we smiled at each other.

"Gregory, and same." He stuck out his hand and I shook it. He held it for a few extra moments. Then he released it, put the Eclipse into gear, and pulled away.

Gregory played reggae music for the ride to the hotel.

"I'm impressed that you seem to know your way around Boston," I said, making conversation.

"Yeah, I have family here, so I have driven here a lot. I don't want to run into anyone, so I booked a room out by the airport," he replied.

"Sounds good to me," I said. I was relieved that we'd also be far from anywhere I might run into my mother. I found it funny that we were both in hiding.

"Are you hungry?" He asked.

"Not really, but we can stop for food if you want."

"Yes. A man's gotta eat," he said.

We stopped at a drive-through and Gregory ordered cheeseburgers and fries.

"You sure you don't want something?"

"Nah." I was far too nervous to eat. Plus, when I got into Gregory's car, I noticed a faint odor that didn't appeal to me. I wasn't sure what the smell was, but it wasn't a fragrance that helped stimulate the appetite by any means.

Soon Gregory had his food and all I could smell was French fries. I held his bag on my lap while he drove and occasionally reached into it to grab fries that he stuffed into his mouth.

"Wow, you must be really hungry." I said.

"Starving." He responded, still chewing as he reached into the bag on my lap again.

"If you dig any deeper in this bag you'll be touching more than a burger," I joked.

He laughed then said, "Ahhh then I better save that till we get where we are going."

After a few more minutes of driving, Gregory pulled his car into the parking lot of a convenience store.

"Let's jump in here and get some refreshments for the room."

"Sure thing." I said, unbuckling my seat belt. We both exited the car. When we got to the door of the store, Gregory held it open for me with a smile.

Inside the store under very bright lights, I got my first good standing look at Gregory. He was a touch shorter than I, about 5'7. He was wearing faded back jeans, a white t-shirt and a black leather jacket. From what I could tell through the jacket, he had a little weight on his belly but wasn't fat. His hair was freshly cut and faded. I got a good look at his face through the glass of a refrigerated door he had opened. His skin was a deep shade of brown that reminded me of gravy. His face was dotted with a tease of a beard and a tiny mustache. I smirked a little.

He ain't the cutest, but he ain't ugly either. I thought to myself.

Gregory loaded the checkout counter with his assorted selection of juice, water, and soda. He added two large bags of chips and a bag of peanut M&Ms to his bounty, then looked at me with a grin.

"Want anything? My treat," he asked.

"Is all of that for you, or are you sharing?" I replied. The words came out sounding snarky. I wasn't sure why.

"Oh I will share, I just don't know what you like so I got what I like," he said.

"What all you have there is fine if you are sharing." I answered.

Gregory looked a little annoyed but seemed to shrug it off as he paid for his items. I wasn't sure why I was being such a jerk. We weren't even at the hotel yet and I could tell I had tried his patience.

I decided to shut up for the rest of the trip to the hotel. I remained in the car while Gregory went to registration for the room key. Then I carried his burger bag in one hand and my backpack in the other as I followed Gregory to the hotel room door. He stepped in first then held the door open for me. I walked past him and switched on the light, illuminating a cozy hotel room with a King-sized bed in the center of it. Gregory closed the door and locked it. Then, as if on second thought, he reopened it, placing the Do Not Disturb hanger on the doorknob before closing and locking it again. There was a small round table with two chairs in the corner of the room. I set my backpack down on one of the chairs and placed his food on the table. Then I turned around and looked at him, unsure of what to say or do next.

Gregory took his leather jacket off and tossed it on the bed along with his overnight bag.

Then he looked over at me and said, "Well hello again."

There was a touch of tease in it that made me laugh. Suddenly I wanted to be closer to him.

"Do I just get hellos all night or maybe there's a hug or some show of affection to go with it?" I said.

Again, the words came out sounding bratty instead of inviting. Gregory rolled his eyes at me.

"Why you being so mean tonight girl? You can't say something nice?"

"How am I being mean?" I argued, taking offense.

"Well, the first words out of your mouth tonight we're basically a threat. You got snappy in the store when I offered to buy you something, and now you are complaining that I said hello. What for?"

His Jamaican accent softened the words a bit as they entered my ears. I realized he was right. I was being kind of a bitch, for no good reason.

"I'm sorry Gregory. It's been a long day and...I guess I'm just nervous."

"As the guy who just worked 8 hours and then drove over 4 hours to be here, believe me, I understand a long day. I'm nervous too. I had no clue what this was going to be like you know. But we are here. We are good. Let's enjoy it, eh?"

"Yes," I agreed. "You're right. How about a do-over?"

"Sounds good. Hi, I'm Gregory. Nice to meet you, Lynn." He stuck out his hand again.

"Hi Gregory," I said, stepping towards him. I took his outstretched hand, but instead of shaking it I tugged him toward me and wrapped him in a hug. My face brushed against his as we embraced, and I felt the tickle of his almost beard against my ear. He hugged me very tight. It felt nice at first.

But, being so close to him, I noticed that I could still smell the odor I had observed in his car earlier. It definitely wasn't cologne. I guessed it was just the way he smelled. I pulled away slightly to look at his face, and that's when he moved in for a kiss. I let the kiss happen. His lips felt very soft as they moved across mine, but I didn't open my mouth. I didn't feel in the mood to make out or do anything else just yet. After all, we had just had what some might call our first argument.

After our kissing didn't turn into making out, or anything else, we awkwardly separated and found our own spaces in the tiny room. I chose the left side of the bed where the table and chairs were, and he settled in on the right side next to the nightstand where the lamp was. I sat down in one of the chairs.

I still had on the clothes I had worn to school that day, and to the dance after. Basically I wasn't getting in the bed with this strange man who I've known for a long time but was meeting for the first time, with my street clothes on. I thought of that funky odor I smelled in his car, and again when he had hugged me. I didn't want to get naked right away, but I realized I would never get naked with him before both of us got clean.

Gregory had already kicked off his shoes and stretched out across his side of the bed. He turned on the TV and was clicking through the channels.

"Hey, I'm going to take a shower," I said. I chose to seize an opportunity to model basic hygiene, and also prepare myself for whatever else the night would entail. I took my bag and headed towards the bathroom.

"I'll leave the shower on for you." I called out at the last moment before disappearing behind the bathroom door, locking it behind me.

I showered quickly, feeling bolder as I washed the days sins down the drain, cleaning the slate for a night filled with new ones. I felt confident that Gregory and I would have sex. Although the sparks weren't immediately flying for me, there was enough there to work with. I wasn't a virgin anymore, but the sex I'd had up until that point could only get better. I figured at the minimum it was something to compare the boy I lost my virginity to, and compare Gina to. I wasn't scared; I was hopeful. I wanted to have sex with Gregory.

I dried off in the bathroom and put on my Mom's lingerie (again) wearing nothing else underneath. It covered enough of my body for me to feel confident but showed enough of my body for me to think I looked sexy. I glimpsed in the foggy mirror at my reflection, blurred by steam. I gave myself an affirming smile.

Okay KishaLynn. Let's go be grown.

As promised, I left the shower running for Gregory.

"Your turn," I said when I came out of the bathroom. I tossed Gregory a clean towel. He popped up to catch it, looking me up and down in surprised pleasure.

"The shower is nice and hot, just like I am," I added.

Gregory laughed and nodded in agreement. He stood up and started to walk towards me, but I redirected him to the bathroom.

"Don't waste water," I said.

"God, you are so mean," he said.

"What's mean about wanting to conserve water?" I said, trying to soften my tone.

Again, his face split into a smile. "Okay. You win that one."

As soon as Gregory was out of sight in the bathroom, I dug the strip of condoms and spermicide I had brought with me from my backpack. I didn't believe in taking chances with safe sex. I brought my own protection, and I insisted on putting it on myself. No way I was going to ruin my life by getting pregnant because a man didn't pinch the tip. I had bought brand new condoms but still had plenty of spermicide inserts left from my first sexual experiences. Those were just a backup in case anything happened to the condom as my first line of pregnancy defense. I inserted one of the capsules, and then strategically placed a condom beneath my pillow.

I poured myself a glass of juice at the table and took a few sips. Then, feeling clean and ready, I finally laid down on the bed.

Soon, Gregory came out of the bathroom, almost tiptoeing, wrapped in one of the white hotel towels.

"Sorry I didn't bring any pretty negligee to put on," he said.

I laughed. He was cuter when he was naked, and clean. I flipped the covers back and invited him to join me in the bed. He flipped off the lamp on the nightstand, bathing the room in the gray shadows of a television playing the dark. He sat down on the bed, still wrapped in the towel, and then shuffled it out from beneath him. It felt like he was too shy for me to see his penis. I understood that. There was a reason I wasn't naked.

Once he was in the bed, I wrapped my arms around him, and we began to kiss. This time he just smelled like a man—a clean man. I opened my mouth to him and began to move my leg up and down his, discreetly searching for his penis with my knee. Once I felt the semi-soft mound of his growing erection, I knew that we were going to have sex, but not at that very second.

I focused on making out with him for a while. He was an average kisser. It was nothing like the sparks that flew when I first kissed Gina. He didn't taste delicious like she did. But, as his tongue darted around mine between my lips, I started to feel moisture forming between my legs, amplified by the spermicide capsule that was beginning to melt inside of me.

Oral sex was not an option for me. Even though we had typed and talked about blowjobs and eating out in explicit detail during cyber and phone sex, I was neither ready to give nor receive oral sex. The thought of putting a penis in my mouth repulsed me. The thought of a mouth licking on my pussy repulsed me even more. I silently hoped he wouldn't ask. But if he did ask, I was ready to say no.

I could feel Gregory's hands fumbling with the buttons on my nightgown. I broke my grip on him to quickly unbutton and remove the lacy white fabric, tossing in onto the floor. Then we pressed back together and resumed kissing, now skin to skin.

I found the courage to reach down and touch Gregory's cock. It had hardened more, but not enough to be insertable. It felt fairly small to me, but I knew it was still too early to judge. I began to slowly rub his penis in my hands, jerking him off the way I would describe during our phone sex sessions. He broke our kiss to moan a little and thrusted his hips towards me.

Soon his cock was fully hard. It was still on the small side, but big enough to do something with, and hard enough to put a condom. I sat up, pulling my stashed condom from under my pillow. I tore it open and expertly rolled it onto his penis within seconds. With protection, I believed it was better to take action than ask for permission first. He didn't protest at all.

Once he was shielded I rolled over into my back and pulled him close to me. He moved into position on top of me between my legs, which I opened to him. He rested himself on his hands on either side of me and attempted to guide his cock into me handsfree. It didn't work.

Even with my legs spread open as wide as I could get them, and with his cock as hard as it could be, we just weren't coming together unassisted. Once it became clear he wasn't going to change his approach, I reached down and grasped the head of his cock, directing it to where my vagina was.

"Come on," I said, "work with me here."

Suddenly he groaned and rolled away from me.

"What's wrong?" I asked, confused.

"Even trying to have sex with you I get an attitude from you," he said, sounding frustrated. "I'm already intimidated enough. It doesn't help that you can't be bothered to say anything kind." His lilted Jamaican accent punctuated the emotion in his words.

"Oh baby, I'm sorry. I didn't mean what I said. I was just...excited. I didn't mean any offense."

"You were never this bossy on the phone," he said, still sounding very offended.

"I didn't realize you were this sensitive. Please, Gregory. I'm sorry. I'll be nice. We're good. We're here," I said, repeating his words from earlier. "Let's just..."

My words trailed off because I wasn't sure what to ask to do at that moment. Attempting intercourse no longer felt like the right answer. I reached over and rubbed his back.

"I'm sorry. I really want to be with you. But we don't have to have sex," I said.

"I want to be with you. I want to have sex too. Can you just...be quiet and let me do it like a man?" He asked.

"Yes. I can do that." I answered. I knew Gregory was sensitive. I understood. It was a trait we shared as Virgos.

"Okay. Come here." He stood up and held his hand out to me. I scooted to his side of the bed and stood up too.

"Sit on the edge there and lie back."

I followed his instructions and lay back.

Gregory parted my legs with his body and then bent his legs down and pushed himself into me, lifting my lower body off the bed with his thrust. I let out of gasp of surprise once he was in me. There wasn't pain. There was just the pressure of a penis, the second that had ever been inside of me. I wrapped my legs around his waist as Gregory doled out several short strokes. He was moaning gently and grasping my thighs on either side of him as he went.

I pressed my arms into the bed and closed my eyes for a few seconds, waiting either to feel some pleasure or for him to be finished. I silently prayed for both. I would only get one.

After a few minutes, Gregory's moans became louder, and his strokes became more forceful. For a moment I was tempted to say something—to deliver a dirty finisher like I would before he popped on a phone sex call. But I remembered my promise to be silent, so I said nothing.

Soon Gregory's moans took on a higher pitch. I knew he would soon be squeaking his orgasm into the air. I contemplated faking an orgasm, but before I could decide, I heard the undeniable squeal of Gregory's climax. I let out a manufactured sigh of pleasure that sounded very similar to a sigh of relief. Next I felt Gregory pull out. I glanced to make sure his hand was holding onto the condom—it was. He pulled it off and walked it over to the trash.

We had sex a second time that evening, this time on the floor. The results were the same. He got it in and got off, but there was no pleasure in it for me.

The next morning, we woke up and just cuddled, making small pillow talk. He seemed satisfied sexually, which was a huge relief to me.

He was a sweet guy and I preferred talking to him to fucking him.

"You know, I have some very strong feelings for you Lynn. I'm glad I get to know you like this," he told me.

I felt a pang of guilt in my gut. I knew I was lying to him about my age. I knew I needed to tell him the truth and disclose that I was 16 years old.

"Hey, Gregory…" I began with a swallow.

"Yeah?"

"I need to tell you something I haven't been honest about with you."

"Oh yeah?" he said, cocking his head towards mine, which was nestled under his arm.

"Yes," I said. I sat up, looked down at him, and took a deep breath. "I'm 16 years old."

Gregory jumped up like I had poured hot water all over him.

"What? 16 years old?" he shouted. I could hear fury in his voice. For a moment I was scared.

"Yes, I'm sorry. I wanted to tell you before, but…"

"Is this a trap?" he yelled. Now his voice had a high pitch. His fury had turned into fear.

"No, Gregory. I'm not trapping you."

"We've been talking for a while. All this time you've been… and we just…I could go to jail! You're trying to ruin my life."

"No, Gregory. I am not. You won't go to jail. I was never here and I won't tell. It's hard enough to tell you this truth but I like you and I can't keep lying to you," I said.

"No wonder I've felt like you've been playing with me this whole time. I thought I was dealing with an adult. You're a child!

That hurt. I felt terrible. Slinking down into the covers, I began to cry.

"Oh, gosh," Gregory said, calming down. "Don't cry. C'mon now…"

"I'm so sorry, Gregory. I never meant to hurt you. I will not hurt you again," I said. I apologized profusely, trying to explain myself.

"I really liked you. I still like you. It was my feelings for you that led me to keep lying, and it's my feelings for you now that led me to tell you the truth. I understand if it means we can't be lovers again. But please, Gregory, I really want to remain your friend."

Gregory sucked his teeth, and spoke in his thickest Jamaican accent, "Friends. How to be friends with a stranger who lies? Get your things. We're leaving. I'm taking you home right now."

I rode next to Gregory in absolute silence. There wasn't even reggae music playing to sooth the thick shame I felt. Gregory's hurt and anger were palpable. The only good I felt was in knowing I had done the right thing to tell him the truth, even if it caused me to lose his friendship.

When we got to Kelsey's apartment, I asked him for a hug. He refused.

"I think I have touched you plenty, thank you very much," he said coldly.

"Okay. You win that one," I said. I collected my bag and opened the car door.

"I'm really sorry, Gregory," I said one last time. It seemed like I had apologized a thousand times.

"Take care of yourself Lynn. There's dangerous people out here who will lie to you and take advantage of you. I would not want to see you get hurt," he said. He wouldn't even look at me. He just stared ahead, gripping his car steering wheel with both hands.

I exited his vehicle, shutting the door behind me. He pulled away immediately.

I didn't hear from Gregory again for months.

By the time I did, I was already dating a man who was older than my mother. When I told Gregory that, he was so angry.

"Are you crazy to be dating a man 20 years older than you? Does he know you are underage?"

"He knows I'm 17, which is, by way, beyond the age of legal consent in..."

Gregory hung up the phone on me.

I never heard from him again. I sent him several emails. He never responded. I never saw him online in instant messenger again. He had blocked my number at home. I didn't dare call him at work. I didn't care to anyway, because I was already dick-sick over this old man who I call This Nigga.

A year later, from my freshman dorm room at The College during spring semester, I searched Gregory's name and birthday online. I found an engagement announcement. He was marrying a woman named Becky. In the photo, a tall, fat, blonde-haired white girl smiled down at Gregory. He was cradling an adorable chocolate Labrador puppy in his arms and smiling at it like he was getting married to the dog.

That serves you right KishaLynn. At least he gets to be happy.

I didn't contact him.

The next time I looked him up, I expected to find a wedding announcement. Instead, I found his obituary. Gregory had passed away from sudden heart failure. He had congenital heart disease that had gone undetected throughout his life. He hadn't married Becky yet. I always wondered why. He'd been born with a broken heart; he had died with a broken heart. Those are the things that remain a mystery about Gregory. He wasn't too great a lover, but he was too great a friend for me. Rest in Peace.

###

SALVATION AGAIN

There were other campus ministries across The Center, all tied to different mega-churches in the area. All of us were called to get feet in seats on Sunday nights and Wednesday mornings, so it's fair to say there was friendly competition amongst them for souls–on that was judged by who had the longest lines for the church buses that came to campus to take us to church and back. I might have just as easily been a part of a different church or campus ministry, but it was New Redemption and Peculiar that sent Arlene to my dorm room door during the Spring semester of my freshman year, so it was New Redemption's bus that I boarded.

As we filed into the building and took our seats in the wooden pews, I looked around and felt surprisingly at home. When the praise and worship began, I rose to my feet, singing and clapping along to songs, even though they were unfamiliar to me.

I recognized the Holy Spirit in the music as it whipped the entire congregation up into a spiritual frenzy. It felt good to let worship wash over my body. It had been far too long since I had lifted my hands in praise to the Lord. When that was done, an offering was taken. I dutifully wrote a check to the church for $10 and dropped it into the gold plate that was passed along by the ushers in the aisles.

Finally, The Bishop, draped in lush purple robes, took the podium.

"There are four forms of love, amen?" He began.

"Amen!" the congregation responded back.

"We have eros love. That's romance. That's sex. That's passion. That's for marriage, amen?

"Amen!"

"We have familial love, like the love a mother has for a child, and love brothers and sisters have for one another, Amen?"

"Amen Pastor, Amen!"

"We have philia love, like that in Romans 12:10 in which the Word of God calls us to "Love one another with brotherly affection".

"Yes Lord, Amen!"

And then, we have the greatest love of all. Agape love. What is Agape love? Agape love is God's unconditional love for all people."

I wrote that down–"Agape–God's unconditional love."

I had never heard of Agape love before. Up to that point in my life, all love was conditional. But as The Bishop continued his sermon, I realized that for the six years I had been saved, I may have been missing out on the best thing about God–His love. I knew about God's salvation–we needed it to be forgiven of our sins, to go to heaven and be spared an eternity in hell. I knew that God had loved the world to much that He sent His son to die for our sins. I knew that if–IF–one accepted Jesus Christ as their personal Lord and Savior, THEN they could be embraced by God's love, and through righteous living, earn heavenly eternity with God in heaven after death. But the IF-THEN made it a condition. Now here was The Bishop telling me at church on an Wednesday night that God had unconditional love for all people. I felt like God was meeting me where I needed to be met, with what I needed most—love. I wasn't alone. My fellow worshippers around me began to riot in praise. I let it wash over me until the Spirit lifted me from my seat. I rushed to the alter when those who would rededicate their lives to Christ were called to come forward. I cried and I confessed. I was prayed for and held. That evening, I got saved again joined the church. I asked Jesus to order my steps from that point forward.

Arlene was thrilled for me. She invited me to the campus ministry bible studies which I started attending diligently every week. Campus ministry was peculiar. Literally, our campus ministry was called Peculiar. It was tied to a scripture in Bible: **Deuteronomy 14:2** includes the verse "For thou art an holy people unto the Lord thy God, and the Lord hath chosen thee to be a peculiar people unto himself, above all the nations that are upon the earth."

At a campus bible study later that week, I learned that the church was offering Vow of Purity classes which culminated in a ceremony dedicating our sexual bodies to the Lord until marriage. I signed up for it immediately. Now my schedule was steeped in ministry. Sunday's were church. Wednesday's were church bible study. Thursday's were campus ministry bible study. Monday's, Tuesday's and Friday's I did personal bible study in my dorm room. Saturday's were Vow of Purity classes.

After weeks of studying scriptures about fornication, I joined a handful of my peers in the basement at New Redemption for our vow of purity ceremony. As I stood before The Bishop in a white dress, and he adorned my left ring finger with a gold ring with a dangling cross charm, I vowed to abstain from sex until marriage.

Technically speaking, I vowed to abstain from sexual relations with a man until marriage. I made no promises about masturbation or sex with women for that matter. And while I knew that the Bible and the church were against both, I was intentional with this vow. I only made promises that I could keep. I was hopeful that I could pray any gay left inside of me away, but I was not willing to give up pleasuring myself. It was the only thing outside of catching the Holy Spirit in church, that helped me feel held inside pure bliss for a moment.

Celibacy was an easy price to pay for peace of mind. I felt both comfort and safety in celibacy. The sex I had in my life to that point in my life had done me no good. I was going to follow Jesus. I didn't know where He would lead me, but I was sure it was in the direction of a love that wouldn't ever hurt me. Finally.

Once I had turned my mind and body away from sex, and towards Christ, I felt called to become a campus evangelist. Going door-to-door recruiting students to go to bible study didn't appeal to me, so I prayed for God to show me other ways to be of service to His will.

That's when I found out about Freaknik.

After a Wednesday night bible study at church, college students were invited to stay and watch a presentation about Freaknik, a local event that was coming up in a few weeks. We were shown video footage of Atlanta streets and parks, packed with people partying. At first, it looked innocent enough, even fun. But as the footage continued, and zoomed in, it became clear why we were watching it. Debauchery shocked my born again eyes.

Reverend Martin took the pulpit to address us as the footage faded to black on the big screens above us in the sanctuary.

"The footage we just watched was taken at last year's Freaknik," he began. "At this so-called Black Family Picnic, attendees are encouraged to participate in "freaking," which some might call dancing, but appears in the video footage to be clothed fornication, non-consensual touching, and in extreme instances, flat out sexual assault of young women and men."

We groaned in disgust collectively with shared outrage. I could feel the Holy Spirit mourning within me.

"Young ladies and young gentlemen, the spirit of God declares tonight that there will be no more Freaknik in this city," Reverend Martin shouted into the microphone.

"In the name of Jesus, we will stand together to end this scourge of sexual brutality and carnality. Who is with us?"

This raised many to their feet, shouting and clapping with him. I was one of them.

My campus ministry's Freaknik protest was my first taste of what collective action could do. I felt I owed a lot to my church, and to God. And, I felt The College owed a lot to God and the church too—after all, our motto declared the school to be for Christ. It was a relief for me to do something to stop what I viewed as serving our young women's bodies up to debauchery and violence. Thousands of church members and campus ministries members met every evening to pray and plot against Freaknik. We posted anti-Freaknik flyers across all campuses and distributed bright orange buttons that read: "I'M NO FREAK. I Have A Higher Standard." Many students actively rejected me when I tried to hand them a button.

I found out that the College Center was sponsoring bus transportation from The College's campus to Freaknik. I found it unacceptable that the same busses that carried us to church on Sunday were being deployed to take students to a dangerous event.

I wrote a letter of protest to The College's administration, asking, "Is The College, whose mottos says it's for Christ, really going to sponsor its students' transportation to their own potential assault? Will you tell their parents that sexual trauma was included with the $45,000 in tuition they'll pay this year? I urge you to stand behind our motto, and stand with over 5000 College Center students, and agree that WE'RE NO FREAKS!" Then, I emailed my letter to Reverend Martin, who distributed it across the campus ministry so others could do the same.

To my surprise, the following week after the letters were sent, The Center announced shuttle transportation would no longer be provided from our campus to Freaknik. HBCU students were the heartbeat of Freaknik. Now, most of them had no easy way to get there.

The announcement felt like a huge victory for me, but the general masses seemed furious about it. My roommates, Darlene and Samantha, were pissed.

"You're ruining a part of Black history," Samantha shouted at me in our dorm room.

"No, I'm protecting Black futures and The College's brand," I replied. "The motto says this school is for Christ—not for Freaknik."

"We'll just find another way to get there," Darlene said.

"By all means. Good luck and be safe," I replied.

When the event date finally came, those with the resources and courage to do so made their way to the Freaknik. My ministry organized a movie night as an alternative event, which was packed with students. Freaknik was poorly attended, as the event had quickly lost both local and political support.

The next day, no one on campus was talking about Freaknik anymore. More importantly, Freaknik never happened in Atlanta again. I earned a reputation as the "killer of Freaknik" that lasted until my freshman year ended and I went home for the summer.

I returned to The College for my sophomore year still devout. I had missed my church during the summer in Boston, but was able to keep up by watching the Sunday services on TV. I had concluded my freshman year at The College by accepting a job as a Resident Assistant. That's how I met my best friend Shine; I was her RA. The first week in the dorms, she had problems with her roommates. As she complained to me about them, and shared that she was an only child, it reminded me of the struggles I encountered with my two roommates during my freshman year. So I let her move into my dorm room where she slept on a couch I had inherited with the room. I was either in church or on duty in the dorm most of the time, and she was in my room anytime she wasn't in class. She wasn't saved, but she eventually started coming with me to church, then to bible study, then to campus ministry. I told her, "You need to go on and get saved." And she did.

When Shine got saved, I was so happy for her. Our relationship grew even deeper because now she was hungry for Jesus and I finally had someone to share that with—an actual friend, not just the church folks (who were "sisters and brothers" but not really "friends").

Shine was my actual friend and once she was saved, we were both Jesus Freaks. We listened to gospel music, and we prayed together, and we studied the Bible together and we never missed church. We skipped class more than we skipped church. When Shine got saved we both just bonded in Christ. And I was so happy. She seemed to have found peace in the Lord. She needed that peace. She had troubled stories of salvation that are hers alone to tell. I understood. I had plenty of my own left to heal.

###

PREMONITIONS

It had been over two years since a man 20 years older than me, This Nigga, had infected me with his fake love and a real sexually transmitted infection during my senior year in high school.

Jesus has healed me of my emotional pain, and I had consciously let go of This Nigga completely. Subconsciously though, This Nigga was prone to pop up in a dream every now and then. That's where I could see his sunken smile, smell his complex cologne, and tremble beneath his teasing touch again. The dreams bothered me. I awoke from them feeling violated and ashamed, again, for having fallen like a fool for a fraud. I also felt sinful and repentant. I wondered if I would ever be as free from This Nigga during my sleeping hours as I knew I was when wide awake.

The summer after my sophomore year, I stopped dreaming about This Nigga altogether, because I could barely sleep. I had moved home to Columbus, OH and was struck with persistent nighttime insomnia. I was often still awake when the birds began chirping outside. I wasn't avoiding sleep to hide from This Nigga in my dreams. Sleep just evaded me. I prayed about it, and eventually went to see a doctor. The doctor prescribed me some a strong sleeping pill, and I found nighttime sleep again.

That's when I had the first nightmare.

My subconscious dropped me into the dusty parking lot of a bar alongside the road of a desolate town. I wasn't clear how I had gotten there, but it was clear that I was at my destination. I slowly began to walk towards the door of the bar. There was no one else around outside—not even any parked cars. But I could feel that there were people inside.

There were lots of people inside. Faces I didn't fully see or recognize beyond knowing that they were there and that they were looking at something. I followed their gaze to the back of the bar. There I saw faces that I very much recognized, and simultaneously, glimpsed what everyone else was looking at.

It was my mother and This Nigga, standing at a makeshift altar in the unmistakable position of a couple exchanging vows, even though they weren't dressed in wedding clothes. No one was.

All I could manage to do was utter the question, "What?"

"You may now kiss your bride," I heard the officiant, who looked like a bartender, say to This Nigga. And then, he leaned in and gave my mother the deepest of kisses, as if he wanted to swallow her face. My mother kissed him back like she wanted to be swallowed. And I gasped in horror, snapping awake.

The vision stayed with me for several days, troubling me at my core. But I categorically dismissed it as a sleeping pill dream.

Then, the following week I had another dream. This time, I was walking up the road to Audrey's house where we had lived my senior year in high school, and where I had first met This Nigga. I hopped up the stairs and entered the front door, then froze in place. There in the dilapidated living room to the right of the entryway, on top of the stained and cat claw-shredded couch, was This Nigga pounding his way into my Mom who was spread-eagled before him. Both of them were sweating, gulping for air.

My response was the same:

"What?"

When I spoke the word, This Nigga turned his head and looked at me. He continued to fuck my Mom, and he locked eyes with me and smiled the smile that used to melt my heart but in that moment, froze it. I jerked awake again, overwhelmed by the sight. I felt sick to my stomach, but I pulled myself together to keep from vomiting.

Because I was so sick, I thought it was something I ate that prompted my dream. And those days, I was eating pretty much anything I could get my hands on.

The final dream was the worst dream of all. It took place in my Dad's house where I was staying, so it felt real. I came out of my bedroom and was startled to find my mother and This Nigga in the living room, unpacking boxes.

"What?" was my sole reply, again.

My Mom looked up at me and responded with a cruel smile. "Ahh, there she is. We just bought this house," she said.

I looked from her to This Nigga and back to her.

"Why?"

My mother replied: "Because you owe me everything."

I looked at This Nigga. "What are you doing?"

But This Nigga didn't answer me. He just stood there holding a box.

Then, my Mom screamed: "Get out of my house, now."

I snapped awake and had a complete breakdown. I left my father's house and went to stay with my Aunt Brenda for a couple of days. I felt completely unsafe at home and needed to be able to rest. I did finally get some sleep, and on the third day, I took the bus back home to my Dad's house. As I walked up Seymour Avenue from Main Street, I noticed there was some kind of police activity up ahead. It looked like it was happening right in front of our house. My pace quickened and my mind raced contemplating what could be wrong. At first I thought my Dad was in insulin shock again–but there would be a fire truck or an ambulance in the street if that were the case. All I saw were police cars. As I got within one block from my house, I could see clearly that the police were indeed surrounding my Dad's house. Even worse, there was yellow police tape stretched across the gate and lawn–*Crime Scene.*

My heart dropped. Who was dead? No one had called my aunt. Was my father alive? I ran up to the house and tore through the crime scene tape screaming, "Daddy?"

His face appeared at the door immediately. I collapsed to the ground with relief.

"Oh baby I thought you were staying at your aunt's. I didn't want you to come here and see all of this."

I shakily pulled myself together and arose.

"What happened?"

"There was a shootout at the house across the alley next door."

The very house I used to go to for daycare when I was little.

"I don't know if it was a drug deal gone bad or what, but at some point they started busting caps. One poor guy ran out the back door, but they shot him as he ran across the alley. He managed to get into our gate and across the yard but…he passed out on the side of the house and died."

I started to calm down knowing my family was okay. But I still felt scared.

"That's why everything is marked as a crime scene," my Dad said. "The body is gone but they are still collecting evidence. They even have the body outlined, just like on TV."

"Did they catch the shooter?"

"No arrests were made. It took the police forever just to get here. I'm sure it'll be on the news tonight. Baby, why don't you go on back over to your aunt's? You don't need to be around all this ghetto ass drama."

He was right. I didn't need to be around it. And from that point, I lost Columbus as home. "*I'm never coming back to live here again,*" I thought. The only neighborhood I had been able to call home all my life, even as my Mom moved us all across the United States, was no longer a quaint, Black middle-class neighborhood. Crack had taken over the area, and crackheads occupied every third house on the short block that ended at the freeway. By this time, the intersection of Main and Seymour on Columbus' east side was a notorious no-go zone. You couldn't even get a pizza delivered because the drivers feared getting robbed or shot. I couldn't believe these were the streets in which I used to play with my cousins during few and far between visits home during my childhood.

For my junior year, I was headed to Los Angeles to attend The Cali College on a domestic exchange program. I knew I had to make things work out in California. It was my chance to escape the sadness of Boston and the horrors of Columbus, without having to return to the misery of Atlanta.

###

THIS NIGGA-PART 3

My junior year in college was probably the happiest year of my life. I was still deep into Jesus, but I had discovered new types of Christians—California Christians, who are very different from the Baptist Christians of the south or the Apostolic Christians of my faith's origins. They led with love and stayed there. Sin wasn't the focus. Salvation wasn't the focus. Love was. They centered God's love for us as we are.

Then I went home to Columbus for winter break of junior year. I didn't go to Boston because while I was living the California dream, I found out that my Mom was unhoused again, living back with Audrey in the home I left for college from. That wasn't a good sign. I was worried about my Mom.

When I would call the house to check on my Mom, Audrey would always answer. And she'd always tell me she was super worried about my Mom.

One day during winter break I called the house to see about my mother, and to my surprise This Nigga answered the phone. I hadn't spoken to him since the day I told him he gave me Chlamydia three years earlier. It was very jarring to be speaking to him again, especially after those horrible dreams I had over the summer about him and my Mom.

"What?" I stumbled on the word, and then continued, "What are you doing answering Audrey's phone?"

"Well hello to you too, beautiful," he responded in his usual silky tone. My skin crawled.

"Fell on some hard times and had to come stay here at Audrey's for a bit," he said.

I immediately felt sick to my stomach. Now This Nigga and my Mom were living under the same decrepit roof.

"Let me speak to my mother," I said. When she got on the phone, she sounded high.

"Mom. Listen to me very carefully," I said. "Stay away from This Nigga. He is not a good person. I don't want you to get hurt."

My Mom's voice was a low and light whisper, "Hi, honey."

"Mom, just promise me you'll stay away from him."

"Okay. I promise, Kisha," my Mom replied, "to take care of myself!" She began giggling, as if she'd taken a hit of laughing gas. Or something else.

I asked to speak to Audrey. She got on the phone and I said, "How long has This Nigga been living there?"

"A few weeks. Same time as your Mom."

When I hung up the phone, my first instinct was to panic. But, I was safe and far from any terrible thing happening in Boston. I decided to put it in God's hands. I just prayed that This Nigga wouldn't take advantage of my Mom the way he had me. I just prayed my Mom would make a good choice for once in her life. I went back to California after winter break and continued living my best life as a college junior in Los Angeles.

Two months later I called the house to wish my Mom a happy birthday. My Mom answered that time, so I couldn't get my usual update from Audrey.

It was clear my mother was high. She has a way of speaking when she's under the influence that I recognize and shrink away from automatically when I hear it in her voice or any voice.

"Happy birthday, Mom," I said.

"Thanks baby." She said, slurring. "I am glad you called, because I need to tell you something."

I felt the sickness twisting in my stomach.

"Okay…"

"Well," she said. "Remember how you warned me to stay away from This Nigga?"

"Yes," said, heart racing. "I remember."

She continued. "Well, I couldn't."

And then she started laughing.

"What does that mean, Mom?"

"Well, now I get why you tried to keep me away from him. Because he told me everything about what happened between the two of you."

Now she was cackling into the phone.

I stopped breathing for a minute.

"Okay. What's funny about that?"

After a long sigh, she said, in a very cruel tone, "Well, he's mine now. And we're in love." Her laughter resumed.

I hung up the phone to the sounds of my mother, high on cocaine, laughing her ass off at having "won" This Nigga and his diseased cock from me.

I wrote Audrey an email and told her everything This Nigga had done to me in explicit detail. He took advantage of me sexually. Emotionally. Financially. I told her I was worried he was a predator. He was dangerous to have around in her home, especially around her 15-year old granddaughter who visited often.

Then I told her what I had learned about my Mom and This Nigga. I told Audrey about the *way* my Mom told me, even though she claimed he told her about us, or whatever his version of it was. I begged Audrey not to support whatever they were doing together. She had her issues, but it was still her house, and she had a choice about what happened in it.

She wrote me back immediately and said: "I knew it. I'll handle it."

My Mom was livid that I told Audrey. She called leaving threatening voicemails calling me all kinds of names saying it was all because This Nigga had "chosen her."

She said she was going to book a flight to California and kill me. I knew she didn't have the resources to do that since God knows where she was living without Audrey's help, and I knew she was drugging every extra dollar she did have with This Nigga. When she started threatening my life I contacted campus security, played them her voicemails and asked the college to block her number (they were hard lines in our dorms) and that finally stopped too.

In that moment, both This Nigga and my mother died to me. I never spoke to or heard or about This Nigga again.

I was completely estranged from my Mom for the next six months.

After the pain of my Mom's betrayal, I threw myself back into the church again. But this time I was out in California with these California Christians, God is Love and all sins are equal. In California, I did not experience the fire and brimstone of my youth. I found a God I really believed could love me in all the ways no one in my life seemed to, especially not own my parents. I was an adult now though. I didn't need mommy or Daddy. If God could really love me, as I was, like these white Christians said he would, "no matter what" then that was enough. I still evangelized but I evangelized differently.

In college, I railed super hard against the sins of fornication and the perversion of homosexuality. After taking the Vow of Purity, I felt it was my calling to rebuke these things loudly in ministry. And there were hundreds of other college kids doing it with me, and we attended a church with 50,000 congregants all doing the same thing.

My whole approach to gay people changed, because rather than seeing that lifestyle as this huge abomination that would have you roasting in hell, I saw it as just another thing God loved enough about these people to forgive, just like he forgives everything we do out of love for us and in exchange for love for him and each other.

Leaning into my new campus ministry in California helped me heal from the pain of This Nigga and my Mom because I got to explain to everyone, and myself, that God's love is always enough, and always there, no matter what.

The California Christians didn't seem interested in rooting out sin and changing hearts. Instead, they chose to focus on inviting souls to experience God's love just as they are. Their preaching didn't tell me how to be or think. It invited me to explore God's truth for myself, drawing my own interpretations from Scripture. I didn't go to church once during my year in California, but I grew closer to God than I'd ever been. It was a radical shift for me. I began to focus less on sinful deeds and more on exploring God's love for me.

My desire for women had been long stifled by years of deep and intentional celibacy. I did not believe it was okay to be gay. However, I began to believe that God still loved those who were gay. And therefore, I should love them too. God's love was that awesome. It was a more powerful tool for evangelism than shame. I helped more people get saved in California than I ever led to the my church altar in Atlanta. I learned I could point God's love at anything and feel better. I wasn't ready to point God's love at my latent attraction to women. I needed God's love to heal my lack of parenting. I felt like I had raised myself and I was tired. So I let God's love replace the love of my absent father and my hurtful mother. His love healed me enough to move forward. In the summer, I left California and returned to The College. I was so happy in California that I almost transferred. I came very close. But at the last minute I knew I had to go finish what I started at The College. And I was curious to go back to campus and start ministering differently—if it was allowed.

###

WHEN THE TOWERS FELL

On September 11, 2001, I had recently and reluctantly returned to The College from my year in Los Angeles at The Cali College. I was forging ahead towards graduation and trying to reconcile the Christianity I had found in California with my return to my home church and campus ministry in Atlanta. I had just celebrated my 21st birthday—if going to bible study with my best friend "Shine" could count as bible study. Shine, at that point, was my closest and only friend. She was from New York.

We had grown very close her freshman year when I was her RA. I evangelized her to the church. I was in LA during her sophomore year. When I got back to The College, it was her junior year. She had changed her major to Religion and was planning to become a pastor. We were inseparable during junior year—even though she lived very far off campus. She either slept on the floor in my dorm on an air mattress most weeknights, and I rode out to her studio in Douglasville on the weekends, sleeping on her bottom bunk bed.

I don't know why Shine hadn't spent Monday at my dorm, but I was alone and fast asleep in my dorm room on Tuesday, September 11, 2001, when my telephone jarred me awake just before 9 am. My phone never rang. I answered it.

Hello?

"Kisha? It's Mom."

"Mommy?" I never called her mommy. I still to this day wonder why that was my response to her when the last time I had spoken to her she was laughing in my face and the last time I had heard her voice she was threatening to kill me.

"Something's happening. I need you to find a TV and turn it on."

I sat up, realizing that the tone of her voice indicated that something was very wrong.

I had a tiny, ancient 8" black and white TV in my dorm that a friend had given me so I could watch the few TV shows I liked back then—Ally McBeal and The Simpsons. I got out of my bed, walked over to the TV, and switched it on.

I saw the North Tower of the World Trade Center, gashed and smoking. My Mom was silent on the phone.

"What's happened?" I asked.

"We don't know yet. They are saying it was a plane crash but…this looks intentional."

As soon as she said that I saw the smallest speck streaking from the right side of the TV, and was stunned to watch live as another plane flew into the South tower of the World Trade Center.

Sounds of screams began to erupt and echo, first through my dorm halls and then into the open window from across campus as my peers were all waking to and watching this terrorist attack unfold on live TV.

And there I was on the phone with my mother, whom I hadn't spoken to in seven months. It was way too much to handle. I didn't know what to do or say. It felt like we were all about to die. So I said the only thing that mattered.

"Mom, no matter what happens—I love you." Then, I hung up the phone on her, and immediately called Mira's number in New York. Surprisingly, she answered on the first ring. All I could do was sob in relief at her safety and plea for her to somehow remain that way before our call ended.

An announcement was made that all students should safely and quickly report to The Chapel. I evacuated my dorm to the chapel with everyone else. I could already feel panic spreading—and the grief. Several people feared their loved ones were dead—many would be right. It was absolutely awful. Cell phones weren't very popular yet but the few who had them we're trying to reach people. I was worried about Shine and her people in New York but she wasn't with me and I couldn't reach her. There was news that more planes had been hijacked. Rumors spread that planes had been taken in every major city. Then the Pentagon was hit. I remember looking up into the sky and feeling like a bomb would fall from it at any moment. I just started praying and kept praying. For forgiveness of my sins. I said the Lord's Prayer from **Matthew 6:9-12** over and over again…

Our Father who art in heaven

Hallowed be thy name

Thy kingdom come

Thy will be done

On earth as it is in heaven

Give us this day

Our daily bread

And forgives us our trespasses

As we forgive those who trespass against us…

And forgives us our trespasses

As we forgive those who trespass against us…

And forgives us our trespasses

As we forgive those who trespass against us…

It just played like a hook in my head.

And forgives us our trespasses

As we forgive those who trespass against us…

And it didn't stop. I knew it wasn't going to stop until I forgave my mother.

So I did.

I forgave her.

I let it all go when the towers fell on 9/11.

###

IF LOVING YOU IS WRONG

I'll never forget what it was like to see Shine again for the first time when I returned to The College's campus my senior year. She practically ran into my arms in the lobby of LLC 1, my senior year dorm. I squeezed her so tightly and we just stood there, holding each other for several moments.

"Missed ya a little bit," she said.

"Missed you even less," I replied.

It was so good to have my best friend back.

Shine had moved off campus, but she was almost always with me. After 9/11, we grew even closer. Some nights instead of sleeping in my dorm bed, I would cuddle with her on her air mattress on the floor. But that only tended to be when either she or I were struggling emotionally. There were several of those moments between us. And nothing ever happened—in fact most of that time in each other's arms was spent praying for each other or singing our favorite gospel songs to comfort each other. It was like that through the fall.

As we got into winter, Shine got a job off campus at the nearby Video Place. She offered to hire me on, and since my course load was light, I started working there too. It was a fun job. The only problem was the long walk to work from campus. And The College is in The Center in Atlanta's West End—it's sketch at best, and the ghetto if you're scared of poor Black people. I randomly went online to see if I could buy a car, and lo and behold, I found a single purple car for sale for a price I could afford. I had credit and a job, so I was pre-approved. Shine drove me to pick this car up from CarMax just before winter break.

Because I had my own car, I decided to drive home to Columbus from Atlanta instead of flying. It was about 10-hour drive. That way, I'd be able to get myself around while at home for three weeks instead of taking the bus everywhere.

Unlike the previous year, that winter break, Shine and I spent every waking second our cell phones would allow on the phone. I do mean every waking second, because back then cell phones were only free on nights and weekends. So we counted down minutes each weekday until 9 pm, and stayed awake talking each night until 6 am Mondays through Thursdays. We were known to have 12-hour phone calls on Fridays and Saturdays. She had access to the internet, but she wasn't online as much as I was, and didn't have her own phone line like I did so we couldn't stay connected that way.

We talked about everything during those late nights on the phone. At school our conversations were mostly centered around religion and spirituality in the context of our personal lives. But these calls, it was like God was on winter break too. So we just talked about our personal lives. We started being honest with each other about what life was like at home. I made regular inventory of my own woes, which included a father who didn't care about me, a mother who didn't either, a grown man who had taken advantage of me, and the fear that I'd never be loved.

Shine and I both shared the fear of being unloved. We vowed to always love each other. No matter what. We promised unconditional love for life. And to show up for each other always when needed. Like the scripture said: "Though my father and mother forsake me, the LORD will receive me." **Psalm 27:10** Shine and I would also receive each other.

Things took a bad turn for Shine at home. She called me frantic.

"I need to leave," she said.

"There's still a week of winter break," I said. "Do you want to just come here?"

"Could I?" She asked.

"Well yes of course. Come here and then drive back to Atlanta with me next weekend."

To my surprise, Shine actually did that. She changed her return flight to Columbus from Atlanta, and the next evening I was picking her up from Port Columbus airport.

I was both excited and ashamed to welcome Shine to my home. The reason for my excitement may be obvious, but the shame comes from the conditions my family were living in in Columbus—and the neighborhood, which I knew to be a *real* ghetto, which was why, even thought it was long, I was never scared to walk to work in Atlanta.

Anyway, I shook off the shame and welcomed Shine into my Dad's dilapidated home on Columbus' east side. I introduced my grandmother to my best friend from college, who was visiting from New York and driving back to school with me. My Dad was happy to meet her because he didn't want me making the drive alone. My stepsister and stepmom were friendly to her. My step niece loved her.

Shine didn't seem to mind the dirt and decay of 626 Seymour at all. She was at ease compared to where she had come from, and I could tell. I was also greatly relieved by her presence, as it created companionship and positive attention for me at home.

In my room at home, I had a twin sized air mattress on the floor for Shine, just like the one in my dorm room, that I'd set up next to my fold-out bed. I spent every moment possible cuddling with Shine on that air mattress. We watched TV and cuddled. We listened to music, cuddling. We talked and cuddled. There was no praying. Both our prayers had been answered. We were together.

Nothing felt wrong or unnatural about this. I didn't even care if we got caught cuddling. My niece would often burst into my room uninvited and unannounced. I didn't jump up or rush to close the door if Shine and I were cuddling. It felt innocent and I didn't care if my family saw or questioned it. I knew what it was and what it wasn't. Besides, none of them ever asked about it.

The remaining days passed quickly, and soon it was time to load up for the drive back to school. It was forecast to snow the day of our departure, so we decided to hit the road at dark thirty to outrun the incoming storm. A snowflake or two fell as I hugged my father goodbye, then joined Shine inside my car which had been running for a while to get warm.

It was an uneventful drive from Columbus to Atlanta, with one distinct difference. Ever since I had purchased my car, I had only played gospel music in it. I said it was God's car, and it was meant for praise and worship only.

On this particular road trip, I pulled out my binder of CDs (I had almost 100 CD in my collection, and I had learned to burn music during my junior year in LA when Napster hit) and played secular music. I let Shine DJ, and we listened to great R&B music and slow jams for the entire drive. The drive had taken all day because we hit snow in Kentucky that lasted until Tennessee, and we stopped to eat a few times.

It was past midnight when we pulled up to Shine's studio apartment in Douglasville that night. We had taken turns driving and were both exhausted. I quickly changed into pajamas and flopped onto my bottom bunk. Shine changed in the bathroom. When she came out, she started to climb the ladder to her top bunk as she always did. While I did sometimes cuddle with her in the air mattress in my dorm, we had never cuddled together at her place.

"Hey," I said, stopping her ascent. "Will you sleep down here tonight?"

It didn't seem like an unusual request. I told myself it was innocent, especially since she'd been sleeping in my arms all week long at my house. But as she climbed under the covers with me, snuggled into her usual position under my arm, and rested her head upon my right breast, I felt something different wash over me. It was arousal. It was desire. Maybe it was the quiet storm of slow jams we had listened to for 10-hours. Maybe it was three and a half years of stone cold celibacy. But suddenly, I wanted more of a touch than a cuddle.

I turned my head to the right. Shine's face was right there, illuminated by a stream of streetlight peeking in through the blinds in her studio window. Her eyes were half open.

"Hey," I said.

"Sup?"

"I love you. More than anything," I said.

"I love you too," she replied.

Then, I leaned in, and I kissed her. I mean, I *kissed* her. There was nothing timid, fearful or questioning about this kiss. I kissed her like we'd been making out forever. I kissed her like a lover. I kissed her like I loved her.

Shine kissed me back. She immediately met the fullness of my passion in kind. As we continued kissing, I rolled over on top of her and caressed her body. Now there was no doubt in my mind what was happening, or about to happen. Pausing our kissing, I sat up and removed my pajamas. Shine removed her shirt and as soon as I saw her tits bounce free in that same streak of streetlight, I dove into them. I grabbed at her and ravished her breasts with kisses.

I realized in that moment as I feasted that it was the greatest feeling in the world to me. It was like I was slathering myself with a woman. All I wanted was more of it. More of Shine. There was no point in stopping. Especially since Shine was in no way stopping me. I lifted my face from her chest to look at hers. She was laid-back, gasping with pleasure. The smile on her face was all the encouragement I needed to proceed. I peeled Shine's shorts and panties off and continued to indulge my mouth in Shine's body from her breasts, down her stomach, straight down between her thighs. Without hesitation, I dove right into Shine with my tongue.

She was hot and sweet on my tongue, and she was so wet that my upper and lower lip were soon soggy with her juices. I didn't care about a single thing in the world except eating her pussy to completion. And when Shine finally came, I came too, even though I wasn't touching myself. That's only happened a few times in my life—that was the first time.

When we were done, we both fell fast asleep and slept until after 2pm the following day.

When I woke up, Shine was cooking breakfast. I thought there would be shame, but there was nothing but joy. And love. And after we ate…more sex. There was never a "wait a minute, what are we doing" moment…we just…got into it. And stayed into it.

That afternoon, Shine made love to me. She went down on me and even though she said she had never been with a woman, I came so hard that I began to laugh hysterically at the height of my orgasm.

"What's so funny?" Shine asked from between my legs.

"Nothing," I answered.

But the funny truth was that before then, I thought only This Nigga person could ever make me come like that. And Shine had proven me wrong.

From that moment on, I knew I was a lesbian.

###

TACO HELL

In the Fall of 2002, Shine and I moved into our first apartment together.

She was a senior at The College and I was a newly emancipated graduate. I hadn't spent a lot of time during college thinking about how I was going to provide for myself. I had been a full-ride scholarship recipient. That had taken care of not only my tuition but also my housing and a lot of my day-to-day needs. Now as a college graduate I had to worry about rent, my car note, car insurance, groceries, and a bevy of other things. I had never learned how to budget or manage money. I just knew I needed to get a job and ASAP.

Fortunately, we were able to find an apartment that allowed us to move in with only a $99 deposit. I had expected that I would graduate with some money but my mother informed me on graduation day that she had spent the money that my grandmother had left me in an insurance policy.

I was angry and I felt violated of course, but at this point I had moved beyond allowing my mother's betrayals to consume me in adulthood. I decided to let it go because not doing so wasn't going to get the money back. It probably wasn't a lot of money anyway. I knew I couldn't trust my mother to tell me exactly how much. I was surprised that she'd even confessed that she spent the money in the first place.

I still had my job at a local video rental store, and that was at least worth something. I knew I needed full-time work, so I started hitting the classified ads pretty hard. I found a listing for a job fair that I attended. At the fair, I met a Black man who told me about a franchise operation that ran several local Taco Places, including the one that was right in front of the apartment that Shine and I had just moved into.

I filled out an application and had my first interview there on the spot. I completed a telephone second interview that same night, where I was offered the job. The salary was $21,000 a year, no benefits, for a mandatory 50-hour work week. That was $8/hr. No one had ever taught me anything about salary negotiation, or about how to calculate whether a certain salary was sufficient to meet my monthly expenses. My paychecks only netted me $650 every other week. I paid my $400 rent, my $195 car note and insurance, and bought gas with my first paycheck. I'd pay utilities, my cell phone bill, and help with groceries out of the second paycheck, using the rest to make my minimum credit card payments.

Shine's Mom was paying her rent, but I was on the struggle bus. I had spent my entire college education on a full-ride scholarship and failed to obtain the most important education of all—financial literacy.

To remedy that, I accepted another "job offer" I received at the same job fair from an ambitious couple who work for an insurance company. They told me they were building a new team, no experience required, and that complete training would be provided. They told me that I could be making up to $10,000 a month.

That sounds good to me. I thought.

This is how I became a life insurance salesperson and a licensed insurance representative. I attended weekly sales trainings, got licensed to sell insurance, and even recruited a small team. I never made a dime on life insurance, but I probably invested a few hundred into it before I got tired of it, charging the expenses to my credit card as an "investment in my future." While I hadn't sold a single insurance policy, I had managed to beg enough people to attend an information session that I had recruited three team members, including Shine and two coworkers, one from The Taco Place and one from The Video Place.

Shine and I agreed to work the business as partners, although I was the only one who ever booked any appointments. I was also over calling people trying to book financial assessments. On my last sales call, I got cussed out by a coworker's wife. Instead of telling me no to my face when I offered him a financial assessment after listening to him complain about the cost of his large family (five kids, which my team leads said was an easier close), he told me to call him that night and talk to his wife about it. She flat out declined the appointment then absolutely laid into me for having the audacity to offer it to her husband.

"How the hell are you, a stranger to me, gonna come up in here and tell me about my money? I know my money. Why are you talking to my husband at work about my money? Talking about you have a business, you need to be minding your damn business and leaving my family alone."

The sound of that woman hanging up on me rang in my ears for about an hour. It didn't stop until I emailed my team leaders and told them I was quitting.

Shine and I were living two different lives during the day. She was a senior at The College, and I was a The College graduate slinging lettuce and cheese at The Taco Place across the street from our apartment throughout the week and shelving DVDs and VHS tapes on the weekend.

Working at The Taco Place was intolerable. My training restaurant had been almost 50 miles away in Carrollton, GA. The gas, the traffic, the long commute we're all soul-crushing, but I adored the people I worked with, especially my training GM manager. He was one of those middle-aged white guys that had just married a beautiful Black woman, so he was cocky and put on an urban tone when speaking to me and my other Black trainee colleagues. Once my training program had completed, I was placed as the Assistant General Manager at my preferred location—right across the street from our apartment. I was eager to start.

Day one at my permanent location, I knew there would be problems. Both the General Manager, Trina, and the existing Assistant General Manager, Jolene, were total bitches to me. The hourly crew was a rag-tag team of Latinos who didn't speak English and one old white guy who had worked there for 7 years and still only manned the drive-thru during the lunch rush.

None of them even acknowledged me on arrival, except Trina, who snapped at me that I was late, even though I was precisely on time. "On time means on the line" she said, alluding to the fact that as a salaried manager I should arrive 30 minutes early each shift so that I could do shift prep things before joining the team on the line at my start time. Just like that, a 50-hour week became a 52.5 hour work week, no overtime.

On my second day, I opened, and the existing AGM closed. She flipped out when I glanced at my watch briefly when she arrived at work. I wasn't even checking if she was late or on time—I just have a habit of checking my watch a lot.

"Bitch don't you be clocking me," She said, lunging my way in a threatening manner.

"I wasn't clocking you," I said, startled at her reaction, but unwilling to be bullied at work.

"Fuck ever," She said before walking away. The whole team on the line watched the exchange, their hands never slowing from the fast-paced work of manipulating tortillas, beans, meat, lettuce, cheese and sauces into a variety of dishes on the menu.

Instead of chastising Jolene for being too late to be early, Trina came from her office and gave me hell for checking my watch as well.

"You so worried about the time. Only time you need to be focused on is *that* time." She yelled, pointing up at the ticket times on the order screen and the speed of service clock flashing at us from the wall. "And stop putting all those damn tomatoes on the tacos. It's 3-4 diced pieces."

I didn't argue with her even though the weight tests we had to do during training proved it took exactly 12 diced pieces to equal the correct tomato portion on that taco.

Day three on the job, I was deemed ready to close on my own, because Trina was off. Jolene opened. She did no pre-shift with me. When I arrived, she rolled her eyes at me and left. I didn't know who was working with me that night. I had the schedule, but I didn't know names and faces. The entire crew ghosted me with No Habla Englaises and dumb blank stares. But they knew well enough to make the food, so I focused on customer service and being the cashier.

My The Taco Place was much busier than my training location which was quite remote by comparison. My training restaurant had been off a rural Road in Carrollton. My home restaurant was in front of a brand-new super Target that had just opened. And it was across the street from a large high school. So, during the day I had to deal with throngs of teenagers coming in, buying $.99 tacos and staying for hours even though they were supposed to be at school across the street.

And at night I had to deal with wrongs and throngs of cars lined up in the drive-through after Target closing delivered me with customers who had worked up quite a hunger while shopping. The holiday season was absolutely crushing. Jolene quit just after Halloween, and Trina put me on a ruthless close-open schedule three days a week, closing the other two-nights and splitting my off days to Mondays and Thursdays so that she could take the full weekends off.

"I need to spend time with my Mom. You don't have a family, plus you live across the street," she said.

She was right. I didn't complain, even though I was exhausted all the time. When I did sleep, I often dreamed of making taco salads and Mexican pizza. And my meager paycheck meant that I was virtually living off free Nachos Supremes and Chalupas. Fortunately, it was my favorite restaurant; I could always eat there happily.

The brutal schedule forced me to quit my job at The Video Place. I wasn't too sad about that—I would miss the free movies but my paycheck were barely $65. Plus, I was dodging a security guard whom I had regrettably made out with one night after the store had closed.

He was cute, with an African accent, so I thought, "Hey why not." But as soon as I felt his tongue darting into my mouth aggressively and his facial hair stretching into my chin I was repulsed by his manliness. It knew it wasn't what I wanted anymore. I even apologized to him for it—but I should have thanked him for helping me see that men were no longer a temptation or attraction for me. If an intelligent, attractive muscular man with cocoa brown skin, a friendly personality, a charming accent and a good job couldn't woo me, no man could.

My team was starting to communicate with and around me in English, which I took as a sign of progress. Most of them were decent people who knew how to dig in when needed and rescue the store from the hardest of slams and rushes. However, a few needed to be handled, especially the white guy who had worked there almost a decade but only ran the drive-thru.

One day I spoke to him. "Look man, you've been working here a long time and you only do one thing—the drive-thru. So you should be my drive-thru specialist and be exceptional at getting these orders out the window. Why isn't that happening here?"

He never had any good answers. He'd just stare at me blankly and then take the next drive-thru order. I knew he had to go. I started writing him up for lateness and break violations. He often look disheveled on shift, wearing dirty clothes and smelling like unwashed man and alcohol. I wrote him up for uniform violations. And he would often fuck up expediting orders out the drive-thru, then get an attitude with the customers who were irate that their orders weren't correct.

After the 5th write-up, backed by a customer complaint to The Taco Place hotline, I made the case to terminate him to the Trina. Then Trina confided in me that she wanted to fire him a long time ago, but he had worked there for years before she started and so she felt bad and let him stay on.

"But he's absolutely terrible," I said.

"Then fire him," She said. "But you be the one to tell him and everybody."

"With pleasure," I said.

I completed the paperwork and ordered his final paycheck to be delivered on his last day on that week's schedule. He was working his regular drive-thru mid-shift (12-4) that Friday. I had closed the night before but thankfully I didn't have to open because I always closed on Fridays.

I arrived at 3:00 and greeted Trina who was already packing up her things to leave early, even though the restaurant was in the middle of a small rush. The white guy was hunched over the drive-thru register, doing his normally mediocre job. Before Trina left for the day, she handed me a folded paper.

"Here ya go. It's his last paycheck. Good luck. I'm outta here." Then she left. I knew she was supposed to stay until four on Fridays but I didn't dare clock her.

The guy got off of work at 4, so I decided to let him finish the shift. I threw on a headset so I could listen to the drive thru orders, washed my hands, rolled up my sleeves and jumped on the line to help clear out the abundance of orders flashing on the screens above. By 3:45 things were calm again. I went into the office to get his paycheck. I wanted to give it to him and cut him loose before he clocked out and dashed.

Just before I called him to the office, I unfolded the paper and glanced at it. His check had been printed out on a business check page. I stared at the amount of it...he worked 12 hours a week. His check was for $126–his pay the week he'd just finished. I stared at the number. It didn't feel right because I worked 12 hours a week at The Video Place and my checks were never over $100. He check was almost ⅓ more than my paycheck and I was a full-time manager. Why the hell was his check so high? He never worked overtime.

I went to the computer and opened the labor system. I never looked at it much because Trina handled payroll. I just did the schedule which hardly ever changed. But I had her password, so I was able to access the report and that's when I learned that the guy I was firing earned $10.50 an hour.

$10.50. That was way more money than I was being paid. For far less work in time and quality.

I grabbed the calculator next to the computer and punched my bi-weekly gross pay into it, then divided it by 53 hours I was working.

$6.25. As a salaried manager I was only making $6.25 an hour. Plus, free overtime. I was enraged.

"Roy," I yelled from the office. "Please step in here."

When he ducked his body into the small office, I didn't hesitate whatsoever.

"You're fired. Here's your last paycheck." I handed it to him, along with the termination notice attached to his final write up for the customer complaint.

He looked more annoyed than stunned.

"Man, whatever," he said. "I don't even need this boring ass job."

"Well, I guess we're both happy then that you don't have it anymore. No need to clock out. I'll take care of that for you, as usual." I said referring to the many instances when he informed me that he had "forgotten" to clock out for his meal break.

He turned and stormed out. I clocked him out then took a moment to compose myself before facing the team and the rest of my shift—one that wouldn't end for another 10 hours by the time finally locked the doors behind me after closing and cleaning the restaurant.

When I finally got home, I collapsed onto my bed, still wearing my uniform apron that was smeared with refried beans. I burst into tears. $6.50 an hour. Four years of college to barely be earning minimum wage at a fast-food job. And the white guy, who did less, was paid significantly more.

I had to do better than this.

I wailed into my pillow and cried until fatigue mercifully put me to sleep.

When I awoke at 2:00 pm, still dressed in my work clothes from earlier that morning, I had made my decision.

I reached for a notebook and tore out a sheet of paper from it. On it I wrote:

"I can't take it anymore. Today, I *quit!*"

I taped the note to our refrigerator, quickly changed into a fresh uniform, and left for work.

The shift was quiet; most Saturday mornings were. Roy didn't work weekends, but everyone already knew he had been fired. I didn't ask how. I liked my weekend crew. They were dependable and expedient. The restaurant opened at 10 am and it took a couple of hours for business to pick up. But the lunch rush at noon came on hard and stayed busy for a few hours. Then there was a lull of steady business until the Target closed at 9 pm and we were slammed again before closing.

After the last drive-thru order was served and the exterior lights switched off, I left my crew to start cleaning up while I sat in the office and input the financials. After I entered all the numbers, I printed the week-end report which was to be faxed to the main office along with the following week's schedule. I laid all of the papers onto the fax machine tray in order. Then I opened the paper tray at the bottom, pulled out a piece of paper, and began to write.

To Whom It May Concern:

I hereby give notice of my intent to resign from the position of The Taco Place Restaurant Assistant General Manager. My last day will be Friday, December 20, 2002.

Sincerely,

KishaLynn

Two weeks' notice. That's plenty. I thought.

I wasn't sure if I meant it was plenty of notice for my employer or plenty of time for me to figure out what I was going to do without a job.

I placed my handwritten note on top of the weekend report, pressed the buttons which started the auto-dial to the main office, and held my breath as the fax machine sucked all four pages of the week-end report through its scanner, followed by my letter of resignation. The beep which signifies its delivery bore the sound of salvation to me. I was quitting my first real job.

The Sunday night shift was uneventful. The office was closed so I knew my notice wouldn't be discovered until the following day on Monday—and I was off. I'd hear everyone's reactions on Tuesday when I returned after some much-needed rest.

Trina confronted me immediately when I walked in on Tuesday.

"You couldn't call me first?" She asked. "I thought we was better than that."

I couldn't fathom how she thought that, but I chose not to argue.

"Sorry. I didn't want to bother you. Besides, I didn't plan this. I just feel this is what I need to do. I'm not happy here and it's not enough money to survive."

She looked at me with disgust. "You ain't even work here long enough to be unhappy."

I could understand her disapproval. She had been an employee of The Taco Place for 13 years, starting as a cashier and working her way up to GM. My last day would also be my four-month anniversary with the company, and I'd only been at that location for ten weeks.

"It's not personal. It's just not working. But don't worry—I'm going to do everything I can in the next two weeks to ensure a smooth transition. I don't believe in checking out. You can still count on me to do my job."

She scoffed at me but remained silent. I dismissed myself to start running my pre-shift checklist.

The next two weeks flew by uneventfully. I kept my promise to work hard until the end. Trina had begun to train Rodney, one of our shift leads as my temporary replacement. The night before my last day, she trained him on closing, and left him with the keys to the store.

When I came into work the following morning, my morning crew was already there opening the store.

"Miss," one of my crew members said as soon as I stepped past the cash registers. "I don't think Rodney finished closing last night."

"What do you mean he didn't finish closing?" I asked.

"We got here this morning, and all the stuff was still on the line. They didn't clean or wash dishes. It looked like they just left."

I immediately panicked as I looked around the store. She was right. Both the hot and cold food stations were packed with food that had sat out all night. In the rear of the kitchen, I saw the dish sink was full. I looked down at the floors, still coated in beef crumbles and cheese shreds.

"Holy fuck. What the hell?" I yelled out loud. Then, it occurred to me to check the safe.

I rushed over to the safe and entered the code that would start the 10-minute countdown to releasing its lock. While I waited, I rushed to help the crew finish the previous night's close and prepare to open for business at the same time.

When the safe timer went off, I opened it and confirmed what I already knew–it was empty. Rodney had taken advantage of having the safe code and the keys to the store and robbed us blind. I inhaled sharply as I put together what the empty safe meant. Then, I rushed to my phone and called the Regional Manager. He didn't answer, so I left a voicemail.

"Hi, this is KishaLynn. It appears we've been robbed by an employee who closed the restaurant last night. Please advise as soon as possible. Today is my last day and I do not know how to handle this situation." I hung up on his voicemail, took a deep breath, and then called Trina.

I don't know how she did it, but Trina showed up to the restaurant in record time. It felt like only seconds had passed before she was storming in the door, screaming, "What happened?" The Regional Manager hadn't even returned my call yet.

Trina was belligerent as I explained to her what had unfolded since I arrived that morning. She burst into hysterical tears. I didn't understand what was wrong–she hadn't robbed the store. Why was she so concerned?

"I was supposed to close. He wasn't cleared yet. I gave him my keys and my safe code. I'm going to get fired for this."

I immediately understood her situation. I felt sorry for her. My sympathy increased exponentially when the Regional Manager marched into the store a few minutes later. Without even greeting me, he stormed up to Trina and fired her on the spot. I couldn't believe it. She had worked her way up from cashier over 13 years and served as General Manager for over a decade. He didn't give a damn. She was told to leave immediately.

Once Trina was out the door, he turned to me.

"So, is today still your last day?" he asked.

"Oh, it most certainly is," I answered. "And not a moment too soon."

###

BREAKING POINT

By the end of the summer after I graduated from The College in 2002, Shine and I had moved out of her studio in Dunwoody, into an apartment near Decatur. She started her senior year, while I used my brand new degree to master the art of squeezing lettuce and cheese into pre-formed taco shells at work before I had eventually quit.

Shine and I each had our own bedrooms in the apartment, but we always slept together. We usually had sex on the futon in her room. But most nights we preferred to cuddle on the air mattress on the floor in my room. After a couple of months, I saved up enough money to buy a real mattress and box spring. From that point on, we slept and fucked in my room.

Our apartment was huge; it was also largely empty. We had no living or dining room furniture. Neither of us cooked and we both hated cleaning, so dishes were minimal. We didn't even have a kitchen table, or a single chair in the apartment. It didn't bother either of us. We had no friends, and no inner circle outside of church. And we certainly weren't spending much social time with church folks. We had each other. We both seemed content with that.

Rather than spend money on our apartment, Shine and I preferred to lavish each other with gifts—expensive tokens of love that we couldn't afford. It started with Christmas. Shine spent a ton of money on me. I felt the need to compensate, so I went all out on Valentine's Day and her birthday. Things peaked on my birthday when she bought me a digital piano I often visited at the local music store. She also bought me a dog—a Shih Tzu mutt that I named "ShangHai"

I was trying to keep up, but while Shine was living off her mother's money, I was maxing out credit cards for my purchases. My entire paycheck was barely enough to cover my half of rent and utilities, my car and insurance, and cell phone bills. I ate and brought food from the restaurant almost every day. Shine would often place her order before she left for school for the day, and I would bring it home after my shift ended.

Shine and I were so happy in love, little else seemed to matter. We were content to be together and in love. We didn't talk about being gay. We were just being. And our unfurnished apartment was the perfect closet for us.

Until the roaches moved in. Four months into our lease, our apartment became infested with enormous flying roaches. They called them waterbugs in Georgia; I called them disgusting and unacceptable. We would find these bugs crawling across the kitchen floor, down the hallway, and on the bathroom walls. While I was often desperate to cleanse myself from refried bean residue after work, I became afraid to take long showers, for fear I would soon be joined and traumatized by one of these despicable winged cockroaches.

We immediately complained to the complex manager. She was a condescending white woman who initially indicated the roaches were a result of our uncleanliness. She came to inspect our apartment herself and found it not only spotless, but damn near empty, except for several roaches, dead and alive, that we counted out to her as we showed her the place. She had to admit that something else was drawing an extraordinary number of the pests into our place. While she continued to imply that the problem "wasn't that bad," she put us up in a motel for two nights while our apartment was fumigated.

When we moved back into our apartment, the roaches were dead, but not gone. We had to clean the carcasses up ourselves. They were found in every room. The fumigator said they had discovered a nest underneath our patio. The bugs were entering through the drainpipes. The thought made me gag. They had removed the nest. After a few bug-free days, we were able to relax again. My long showers resumed.

But things started to change with Shine as she neared graduation.

We were still sleeping together, but less.

Sometimes she slept in her own room.

I worked as assistant general manager of The Taco Place right across the street from our apartment.

I thought maybe she didn't want to smell tacos while she slept.

One day I come home from work on my break to change pants because I had spilled beans or some taco-type-shit on them. Shine's car was parked in the space, so I knew she was home.

She was supposed to have class.

I found her in her bedroom, sitting in a bathrobe. Fresh out of the shower.

"What are you doing home?"

We asked each other at the same time.

Except I had a good reason—to change pants. What was hers?

"Not feeling well?" I asked.

"No, I'm good." She said.

"Okay," I said. I started to back out, but something felt off.

And smelled odd.

I noticed her hair was still glistening from the shower.

"Is someone here?" I asked.

"No." She answered.

Pregnant pause. She wasn't looking at me.

I took a step into the room and noticed her bed had fresh sheets on it. Rumpled sheets.

"Was someone here?" I asked slowly, measuring my words with steady breaths.

"Yeah."

I inhaled the air. Now I recognized the smell.

It was weed, which Shine and I never smoked. It was cologne—and not Shine's signature fragrance of Cool Water. In an instant I knew—it was Johnny.

Johnny was the maintenance guy at our apartment complex. He was Black, huge, and loud. He roared around the complex in a large red Ford pickup truck, blasting music and hanging out of the window as if he was so fat his entire body couldn't be held within the massive vehicle he drove. We could always hear Johnny coming. He often cracked inappropriate jokes, but I tolerated them because he was funny as hell. Also, he would fix shit for us in the apartment without us having to go through the property manager who was a fucking bitch.

But Johnny moved slow on projects, so he was around more often than I would have liked.

"Did you fuck him?" My voice cracked with the pain of the answer I already knew, watching her sit there in her terry cloth bathrobe that I bought her for Christmas while the suds from her shower still burst at the nape of her neck from the betrayal she tried to wash away.

"Yes," she said. The word hung in the air for a moment on its way to me. I was tempted not to catch it; to take the whole question back, to hell with its answer, change my pants and get back to slinging bagged meat, lettuce, and cheese across the street like nothing ever happened.

But I had to receive it.

I felt like I could no longer stand, so I sat next to her on the bed and we both hung our heads in a complicated silence.

She spoke first: “I’m sorry.”

“For what?” I said, trying to remain calm. “For fucking the maintenance guy?”

She didn’t respond.

“I didn’t even know you liked him.”

“I slept with him out of curiosity. It’s been a while. I wanted to know what the dick was like.”

“And?”

“He wasn’t shit.”

“Oh.”

There was a slight retch in my gut at the thought of him naked, massive in height and size, laying mediocre dick in my best friend and for the past year and a half. Each breath I took, I inhaled his disgusting cheap cologne.

I stood up.

“Well, thanks for not bringing him into our bed. I mean, my bed.”

I took a few steps back towards the door.

Before I left the room, something compelled me to add...

“Hey, you’re free to do you, you know. Just…” I paused, carefully choosing my words. “Just don’t expect to do me anymore.”

I turned and left.

As I was exiting the apartment parking lot, Johnny came in his truck turning in on the opposite lane. His window was only partly lowered, enough to see his forehead, shiny with sweat, and his dark eyes give me a flirtatious wink over my own reflection glaring back at him in the glass.

Fuck Johnny.

He may have gotten what he wanted from her.

Or given her what she needed.

But he didn’t stand a chance with me. And neither did she anymore.

My heart was broken, but I didn't cry. I knew what I had with Shine couldn't last forever. I was blindsided by Johnny. I didn't think Shine and I were anywhere near over. My only problem was that we were secret, Christian lesbian lovers. I just wanted to be lesbian lovers who were Christians. But Johnny had ended my lesbian love affair with Shine because she wanted a man. And I realized that I just wanted to be out as a lesbian, because I never wanted to be with a man again.

###

OUT OF THE CLOSET

Shine and I had ended our brief but sweet secret lesbian love affair. It was secret because, I was, we were Christians. And I mean like, Christian, Christian–evangelical, tongue-speaking, foot-washing, holy oil-flinging, church shouting, hands on praying for you, scripture quoting Christians. So, the fact that we found each other sexually and romantically was a coincidence with consequences that came and went.

But suffice it to say that our moment of being lovers was over, and we were back to just being best friends, and roommates, and kinda Christians. Church attendance dropped significantly when there was no bus to get you there every Sunday and Wednesday, and there weren't hundreds of other students eyeballing to see if you were in attendance. Shine tended to not miss church, but I stopped going as often.

The summer came and Shine graduated from The College. After she collected her degree, she got a summer job working with her mother back in New York, and that left me alone to my own devices for eight weeks. I started thinking about where I was and where I wanted to go next in my search for love. It had been three months since Shine had slept with Johnny and our love story ended. But I wasn't finished looking for love. And I knew I wanted to find it again soon.

I felt a burning desire inside to reveal myself to someone who knew me. The thought of coming out to any of my family members was terrifying. Coming out to my friends was impossible. They all knew me as an evangelical, fundamentalist Christian. They didn't know my secret and I knew that they would judge me. It was part of the job of our religion.

I thought long and hard about who would be the safest and how I'd let them know. I decided that I would approach coming out in tiers.

The first tier was to come out to myself.

Is this really who I am? Is this the direction I want to go? Can I even call myself a…lesbian?

The answer was quick and clear. *Yes.*

Once I had that answer for myself, I continued to the next tier--God. I closed my eyes and I prayed:

Dear God, I truly love you. I have asked for a lot in my life, and you have provided in accordance to your will. Jesus, I come before you with the biggest ask of all.

Is it okay for me to be gay?

YES.

Could it be that you made me this way?

YES.

If it isn't okay for me to be gay

Answer my prayers and take it away

Is it a sin?

DID I TAKE IT AWAY?

Is it okay for me to be gay?

Once again, a quick and clear answer from the depths of my spirit:

YES.

I opened my eyes, and never shut them straight again.

Next, I decided that I was going to explore what it meant to come out as a lesbian. I mean, it wasn't a huge leap, considering that

I had already taken a face dive between a woman's thighs when I was sixteen years old. But to identify as a lesbian? What did it mean? *Les*bian?

The more I thought the word and said it, the more I began to fall in love with it. It started to feel comfortable. I had never really let myself try it on before. My church wouldn't allow me to. But this was different now. I was ready to take a first step out of the closet. But what was a logical step–I had by then indulged in plenty of sex with Shine. I didn't want more pussy. I wanted something else. I wanted to connect with other lesbians.

So, I went to the place where I felt most comfortable exploring life and myself–I logged onto the internet. There were surprisingly few search results that popped up when I typed "Lesbians in Atlanta" into Yahoo in 2003. This was during the George W. Bush administration though, so I guess it wasn't that surprising after all. Most of the results were porn. Again, I wasn't looking for sex. I kept scrolling and found an advertisement for a women's Coming Out support group that was meeting up in town the next day. I decided I was going to go.

The meeting was in a recreational center. There was a conference room in the back of the building. I walked through a large and empty main room and entered the conference room. There a group of women of various ages and shades of white sat around a table. I filled an empty seat at this table feeling very large and conspicuous. But I was relieved to be the only Black woman there, because I was afraid to bump into someone that I knew, and I wasn't ready to face the Black gaze as a lesbian just yet.

Once I had taken my seat, a thin woman with blonde hair and gold glasses stood up and began the meeting.

"Hi everyone," she said enthusiastically. "Thank you for joining us for our Women's Coming Out Support Group. My name is Janice, and I am tonight's facilitator. We're going to begin with an icebreaker question. We'll each go around the room, say our names and answer the question: "If you were a vegetable, what kind of vegetable would you be?"

For some reason, I panicked. *A vegetable? What the hell? I didn't come to talk about being a vegetable. What kind of question is this? Is this what white people sit around and do? Is this what lesbians do? Vegetable? I don't know. Would I be corn? Because corn is like, a vegetable so it's good for you but it's a starch because it's bad for you. So are you even allowed to have corn? Is it okay? Oh my God, I don't want to talk about being a vegetable. I want to talk about being…"*

Silence interrupted my racing thoughts, and I realized all the women at the table were staring at me, because it was my turn.

"Oh, sorry," I said. "I didn't realize it was my turn already."

"That's quite all right. What's your name and what kind of vegetable would you be?"

"Thank you for repeating the question," I said, feeling like my tongue was sticking to the roof of my mouth as I spoke.

"My name is Lynn. And, if I were a vegetable then I guess I'd be a lesbian one."

###

UNFETTER:
A POEM TO MY MENTOR

My Mira; My Mirror
Tremendous force of
love in my life
accepting and warm
caring and steadfast in commit
mentoring me through the ups and downs
pushing through to deeper layers of
who I am and still
always
loving.

Grateful is my heart
yet
cleaving to a part that is unseen
maybe felt
but still unseen
unspoken

Truly I say to you that
I trust in you and I believe in
us enough to unfetter my heart
that you might know
as I now know
and continue to know each day

Who
I
Am
a
Lesbian.

Crystal clear
and no longer doubting is my state
of mind and despite it all
despite This Nigga
despite mother
despite father
despite myself
despite even Jesus
it has always been this way
even as a child
and refuses
refuses
refuses to be denied any longer.

Every woman I've ever loved
a shameful secret
Every man I've ever loved
a lie
to myself
and to everybody else.

Lest this truth be cast from me
as a part of God's divine will,
though no condemnation exists from Him
and I pray not from you
I shall live in truth
and the truth has made me free
to love
her.

###

NO EASY EXITS:
A 10-MINUTE PLAY

Trigger Warning: *This play depicts self-harm.*

CHARACTERS:

KL: 23-year-old Black female. Friendly, feminine, and flirtatious.

Shine: 22-year-old Black female. KL's best friend and roommate. Stud with feminine edges. Short in stature but big in Jamaica Queens New York personality. Acts hardcore but extremely sensitive.

Christine: KL's date. 25-year-old White girl. Hippie vibes.

SCENE 1

SETTING: Atlanta, GA. Piedmont Park. Early September. 10 pm.

AT RISE: The stage is set as a nighttime park scene. Streetlights illuminate the pavement. There's a bench that seats two people set at stage right. Trees are projected onto the background.

(KL and Shine enter in the middle of a conversation and begin a leisurely stroll around a short curve towards stage right.)

SHINE

I'm glad to be back home in the ATL. I love Jamaica Queens, but Mama Jane is a tough boss. She worked me like a slave all summer long.

KL

Ha. Well, you have to earn your keep somehow. After all, she is still paying your rent, even though you graduated from Spelman in May. Meanwhile, I'm a year out of school and still struggling to make my ends meet. Count your blessings.

SHINE

True that. Still, I'll take Mama Jane over Boss Jane, all day, any day.

KL

Hey, remember this spot? Valentine's Day last year?

SHINE

Yeah. We had a picnic… *(points upstage towards the trees)* right over there.

KL

A *surprise* picnic. Remember the blindfold?

SHINE

Oh, I remember the blindfold. And how you left me standing on that street corner unable to see for God only knows how long.

KL

It was only a few minutes. Stop exaggerating. I had to set up the picnic. Anyway, wasn't it worth it when you saw the spread? I mean come on—a surprise picnic in the park for Valentine's Day. How romantic is that?

SHINE

You're right. You were a great Valentine.

(KL takes a seat on a nearby bench, Shine sits next to her.)

KL

Remember that night at the Westin? Top floor?

SHINE

Whoo. How can I forget? That view was incredible.

KL

That heavenly bed was incredible. You know, I think that's the first time I've ever fogged up the windows in a hotel room having sex.

SHINE

Yeah...we was wild.

KL

We were more than wild. We were in love.

SHINE

I still love you. *(pause)* So what have you been up to all summer long?

KL

Mostly work. My job at the real estate company is pretty crazy so the time flew by. It hardly felt like summer at all. Although, I did find some new hobbies like going to open mic nights and stuff like that. I don't really have a lot of free time.

SHINE

Yeah well, neither do I, now that I'm back from New York. They are already putting me back on the schedule at the recovery center. I'll be on overnight shifts again.

KL

I'm still mad that you basically get paid to sleep and babysit grown women.

SHINE

Grown women recovering from domestic violence. And who are you to judge?

KL

I'm not judging. I'm just saying. The residents have to stay in their rooms after 9 pm. You work from 10 pm to 6 am. So what do you really do all night?

SHINE

I sleep.

KL

Exactly. *(gives Shine a playful shove)*

SHINE

So, that's all you did this summer? Work and go to open mic nights?

KL

Well, no. I made a few new friends online. Went dancing a few times. It was cool.

SHINE

Get to church any?

KL

Yeah...a few times. But not lately.

SHINE

I never missed church. Hard to skip out on Sunday service when the church is literally across the street from the house.

KL

I know. Oh, and it's a good church too. I remember our first time going last winter. There's nothing better than a tiny, old-school, Black church in Queens. That praise and worship team is the business.

SHINE

Yeah, that choir director don't play. Well, he "plays" *(bends wrist)*...but not on Sunday mornings and NOT on Wednesday nights *(snaps fingers)*.

KL

Amen.

(The two laugh together for a moment, then there's a brief silence.)

KL

Hey Shine, I have something I need to tell you.

SHINE

What's up?

KL

Well, another major thing happened this summer. I've decided I'm ready to be in a romantic relationship again.

SHINE

Oh yeah? With anyone in particular?

KL

Yes and no. You see, my next relationship will be with another woman.

SHINE

Wait, what? What are you trying to say?

KL

I'm trying to tell you that I'm a lesbian.

SHINE

(jumps up) Awwwww hell naw. You ain't no dyke.

(Shine begins to walk away. KL sits there stunned for a moment, then stands and follows.)

KL

(shocked) Wait a minute. Shine. Get back here. You can't just call me a dyke and walk away. That's not how this is supposed to go. Why are you so mad?

SHINE

(angrily) I'm not mad. You just ain't no dyke is all.

(KL and Shine begin to walk a slow loop around the stage's park setting)

KL

You sound mad. Though I can't see how. You didn't have a problem with me being a lesbian when we were together.

SHINE

That was different. We weren't lesbians. We were just in love.

KL

No Shine. I mean, yes I was in love with you. But I was a lesbian. I am a lesbian.

SHINE

(shouting) Stop saying that.

KL

(raising voice) I can say that if I want to. I'm a grown ass woman. Besides, this isn't about you. It's about me. Wanting to be happy. Wanting to tell my truth.

SHINE

Truth. I thought you was a Christian and that Jesus was your Truth. Now you bugging talking this gay shit. You going straight to hell with that.

KL

(loudly) First of all, don't act like we weren't having sex before and after church for many months. Second of all, I am still a Christian. Third of all, I'm gay. It's no less of a sin to lie about it. You already know you weren't my first woman, and you won't be my last.

(KL stops walking. Shine keeps going a few paces, and then stops and spins around)

SHINE

Wait a minute...are you seeing someone?

KL

I've been on some dates. Nothing serious, but...yes, I've met a girl.

SHINE

(yelling) Are you kidding me right now? How could you do this to me?

KL

What am I doing to you, Shine? We're not together. We haven't been together for four months. You're still my best friend but you're not my lover anymore. Don't I deserve love? To be happy?

SHINE

Not with another woman. Naw, fuck that.

KL

This is unbelievable. You're a real trip. At least I didn't do you dirty like you did me this spring. I mean, sleeping with the maintenance guy? In our apartment? Do you know how much that hurt me? Do you know how embarrassing that was to see him smirking around the complex after that? We had to move. But I let you be you. Now who the hell are you to tell me who I can and can't be with?

SHINE

If this is your way of getting back at me for Johnny...

KL

I don’t give a damn about Johnny. Again, this isn’t about you at all. This is about me being who I am. Who I’ve been. I’m really hurt that you are reacting this way.

SHINE

(yelling) You don’t know anything about hurt. You just mad that I got some real dick, so you run off and become a dyke.

KL

(yelling) You didn’t seem to be missing a real dick when my head was between your legs three times a week. But you can have all the real dick in the world if you want because I’m done with dick. And Shine, I swear to God if you call me a dyke one more time then I’ll be done with you too.

(pause)

SHINE

(calming down) I mean, KL...this is wrong. I love you but I’m not gay.

KL

I’m not saying that you are.

SHINE

What we had wasn't gay.

KL

I'm not saying that it was. Whatever it was, it's over now. It's been over.

SHINE

(Shaking head) You can't be gay. You just can't.

KL

(tenderly) I can. And I am. I promise it doesn't change how much I love you. I will always love you. You're my best friend. I'm simply asking you to love me as I am.

(KL reaches out for Shine's hand; after a hesitant pause, Shine takes it. KL pulls Shine into a hug. When the embrace ends, they stand in silence for a moment. Shine is looking down unhappily.)

KL

It's late. Let's go home.

(KL and Shine exit stage left together)

SCENE 2

Setting: Two months later, early November in Atlanta. It's 7 am at KL and Shine's apartment complex exterior doorstep at stage left. At center stage is the apartment interior hallway containing a bathroom entrance with visible sink and medicine cabinet, then a closed bedroom door. At stage right is the entrance to another bedroom. We can see its darkened interior.

(KL and Christine enter and stop at the footing of the entrance to KL's apartment.)

KL

I had a great time last night. I'd invite you in, but I'm expecting my roommate home for her night job shortly. She's still tripping a little over this whole lesbian thing. She's not taking it well that I'm dating a woman.

CHRISTINE

It's cool. I'm just glad it didn't stop us from spending our first night together at a hotel. I hope things get better with her soon.

KL

Yeah me too...at least better enough for me to have you in my own bed.

(KL pulls Christine close and the two kiss each other at the doorstep.)

KL

Thanks for the ride home. I'll call you later. Drive safe.

(Christine exits stage left as KL pulls out her keys and mounts two small steps to her front door. As she goes to unlock the door, she finds it unlocked and slightly open. She enters the apartment into the hallway.)

KL

Shine?

(KL passes a closed bedroom door. She knocks twice.)

KL

Shine? You in there? You left the door open.

(When there is no answer, KL continues down the hallway and stops at the bathroom, noticing the light is on and the medicine cabinet is open. KL steps into the bathroom and closes the medicine cabinet. There are words written on the mirror in red lipstick.)

KL

(reads in a slow whisper) "DYKE BITCH I LOVED YOU." What the hell? Shine.

(KL hurries out of the bathroom and continues down the hall through the bedroom entrance at stage right. She switches on a light to illuminate her sparsely furnished bedroom where Shine is passed out on her bed. A pill bottle lies empty on the floor. KL rushes over to the bed.)

KL

Shine? (*Screams*) Shine!

(KL checks Shine's pulse and listens to her chest.)

KL

Okay, okay you're alive. Shine. Can you hear me?

(KL slaps gently on Shine's face. Shine does not respond. KL pulls out her cell phone and dials 911.)

KL

(into phone) Yes, I need an ambulance right away at 404 Montclair Avenue Apartment 8. My roommate has taken some pills. She's passed out on my bed. Yes, she has a pulse. Yes she's breathing but I can't get her to wake up. (*KL rushes to pick up the pill bottle and reads label.)* There's an empty bottle of

Percocet. No, I don't know how many she took but the bottle is empty. Just please send help, now.

(KL hangs up the phone and tries again to awaken Shine.)

KL

Shine wake up. Oh God please. What have you done? Shine. Can you hear me?

(Shine remains unresponsive. KL picks up her cell phone again and dials another number.)

KL

(crying) Mama Jane...it's KL. I'm calling about Shine. I think she took an overdose of Percocet. She's passed out. We're at home. An ambulance is on the way to take her to the hospital. No, I don't know how many she took.

(We hear faint sirens growing closer in the background.)

KL

Do I know what's going on? I don't know. Well, you see we… I mean, I'm… Oh God. *(crying)* I have something I need to tell you...

END PLAY

GOING GREEN

I checked Shine into a psychiatric hospital after her suicide attempt. Her family came down from New York, packed up her things and moved her out of our apartment. Her mom had begged me for answers about what was going on with her daughter. It didn't feel right for me to tell her about our sexual relationship. The best explanation that I could offer was that I had told Shine that I was a lesbian, and she hadn't taken the news well. I refused to out Shine, or try to explain her attempt on her life. I didn't even understand it. I just knew I wasn't healthy for her, and she wasn't healthy for me. That was enough for me to let go of her completely.

I asked her family to take our dog, Shanghai, with them when they left. They agreed that it might help Shine's recovery. I was glad to see everything go. I broke our lease and transferred into my own one-bedroom apartment in the same complex. My girlfriend Christine and my dear friend Savannah helped me move my few items to the new space. I had recently met them both online.

One month later, I was leaving my apartment for work one morning when I noticed a flash of yellow out of the corner of my eye. There was something large stuck on top of the parking gate. As I began walking towards my car, I noticed that the yellow thing was moving. It was a person. The closer I got to the gate, the clearer I could make out what was happening. I stopped in my tracks. Shine was climbing over the parking gate to my apartment complex.

In that moment I was uncertain what to do. My car was 50 yards away; my apartment door, just slightly closer.

What does she want? What is she going to do? What should I do?

I didn't want to alert Christine, who was still asleep in the apartment. I didn't want to call the cops. I didn't want to be trapped there in an encounter with Shine. I decided to make a run for it and continue on my way to work.

I walked quickly towards my car, glancing every few steps to watch Shine struggling to shimmy over the gate. By the time her feet touched the ground, I had made it to my car. But, she has also spotted me.

Kish…

I do not let people call me Kisha. Shine knew that because I told her, and I told her why. She agreed not to call me Kisha. Instead, she started calling me "Kish", which rhymes with quiche.

"Shine, that's even worse than Kisha."

"But it ain't Kisha tho."

From that point on, she called me Kish and I didn't protest, even though I absolutely hated it.

"Kish…kish. Kish. I swear to God Kish open the door Kish. Please open the door. Kish *open this door or I will break it down and kill you and that bitch before I kill myself.*"

I called the police.

By the time they arrived, Shine was gone. Christine and I explained to the cops what happened. They suggested that I file for a temporary restraining order—Christine too since Shine had directly threatened her. I did that the next day. I never wanted to see Shine or hear from her again. Not because I was scared she would hurt me but because I knew that she would hurt herself. I didn't want her to kill herself, or try to, again. But I also couldn't love her anymore.

I told myself the safest thing to do would be to cut her off. The police tried to serve Shine's restraining order at her job, but the people at her job protected her, like any good social justice service would. However, that tipped Shine off that I had filed one against her. She continued calling and leaving messages on my cell phone and at work. Every number I blocked, she'd find another to call one. Same with email. It really began to wear me down mentally. I started having panic attacks. I was always looking over my shoulder. I was triggered by the ring of the phone and a knock on the door. The only thing that helped me feel safe was my girlfriend Christine's constant companionship at home.

After I got the restraining order against Shine, I was mentally and emotionally wrecked. I had little expectation that she would heed the temporary court order to stay away.

Why won't she just let it go? Please let it go.

Anxiety pillaged my dreams at night. I began to have panic attacks that roared through my ears like a steam engine. Or I would hear the sound of constant gunfire. These excruciating sounds seized my breath and sealed my eyes shut. Unable to awaken or scream or move, I simply had to wait for external interference for the attack to break. Fortunately, my girlfriend Christine was always nearby to shake me awake and love me back to a calm state. It was another reason I was glad she stayed.

My fear of the terrors that awaited me at night were also destroying my days. I became jumpy and easily intimidated by sudden moves and loud noises. I felt on the verge of panic all the time. It was a total absence of peace. But I had a job to do, managing a commercial real estate property in downtown Atlanta.

One day I was surveying one of the properties with a landscaping company. My boss had asked me to get quotes for clearing the brush behind the building. The building sat in front of train tracks, and a few times a day a shipping train would blow by carrying various goods to unknown places. While my landscaper walked the wall to assess the small jungle growing along it, I glanced down the track to look for a train. We were in no danger of being hit by any trains, but I knew I wouldn't be able to handle the loud noise. I hoped he finished up before the next train to whereverland screamed by. Then, in the distance I noticed two fast-moving shadows rushing in our direction along the brush. I didn't have great vision, or glasses at the time, but it only took a few more seconds for me for recognize what those shadows were.

It was a white cop, holding a leash. On the end of the leash, was a German Shephard, which I could now hear barking. My heart froze, but my mouth managed to form words to call the landscaper, who was also white, over.

"Hey." I yelled out to him. As did, I could hear the officer shouting at me to put my hands in the air. My eyes seemed to be the only part of me capable of moving, and they widened to a straining circumference. The officer, whom I could clearly make out now, had his hand at his hip on his gun. The dog, jerking aggressively on the leash, barked and growled. I suddenly felt faint and realized I was holding my breath.

Breathe KishaLynn. Breathe, or you will die right this instant.

I took a gulping breath in that moment, simultaneously launching my hands in the air. I didn't know what I was surrendering to, but it wouldn't be death on that day.

"What are you two doing back here?" the officer demanded.

The landscaper had appeared at my side and had also raised his hands.

"I work here" I blurted out.

"Why the hell do you have a dog on us?" The landscaper demanded.

White people.

I looked at the landscaper like he was crazy.

"This is private property," the officer said. But he also relaxed his hand and ordered his K-9 partner to sit.

White people.

"Yes sir," I replied. "I manage this property. He is my contractor. We are just back here looking at the landscaping for a moment."

The officer seemed to be processing the information that the white guy worked for me and not the other way around. I glanced over at the landscaper, expecting him to validate my explanation.

"We have every right to be back here. What are you gonna do, shoot us?" He shouted at the officer.

Fucking white people!

"I'm going to need to see your ID, and proof that you work at this location." said the officer.

"Officer that documentation is in my office. I didn't bring it out here because we were only coming out for a moment, as we have done many times. If you need to see it, then I need permission to go to my office and obtain it."

The landscaper now abandoned his hands-up position and placed them on his hips.

"This is outrageous. What precisely is the crime here? Why are you questioning us?"

He's gonna get me killed.

And actually, the police was only questioning me, but I didn't say anything because unlike the landscaper, I knew to keep my mouth shut.

"We have been monitoring this area for gang activity and vandalism. The train tracks are government property. No trespassing is allowed."

"What the hell trespassing are we doing on our own property? Do you see any spray paint cans in our hands? We are back here because we have a job to do." The landscaper replied.

Now I was starting to feel grateful. If I just shrink myself and hide in this shadow of white privilege, I, a gay Black woman in the south, might just survive this unfortunate run in with Georgia County's finest Sherriff and his trusty K-9 tag-a-long. I prayed a small prayer, hands still high in the air.

"You may go retrieve the paperwork that proves your right to access this area," the sheriff said.

"You go, I'll stay," the landscaper said. He could see in my eyes that I wanted to get the fuck out of there.

I dropped my hands and scurried through the large fence hole we used to access the back of the building. I walked diagonally across the parking lot towards the main property.

The shortest distance between two points is a straight line. Move it.

As soon as I was out of eyesight of the white officer, his brown dog, and our indignant white landscaper, I blacked out and became trapped in my nightmare of sounds. It was the first time it happened in broad daylight, while I was awake.

I only know what happened from the recounts of my coworkers afterwards. When I came back to myself, I was sobbing on the floor of the women's room in my office building. Tears blurred my vision for a moment, but I sensed immediately that I wasn't alone. I crouched on the floor putting my head between my knees and cried out: "Please don't shoot me."

Vivian kneeled, and spoke to me in a calm, soothing voice:

"KishaLynn, it's okay. You're okay. You're safe."

Then, she sat down on the floor and comforted me with gentle touches on my back until my desperate flood of tears ran dry. Suddenly I was experiencing sensations other than the horrible sounds of nightmares. I could feel the cold floor beneath my knees, and the pain of the tiles pressing into the skin there. I could smell the organic green floor cleaner my boss insisted we use exclusively on the property. I could taste the salt of the pool of tears that had trailed down my face during my massive panic attack. When I felt my eyes could handle it, I risked a peek up at the light, and instead I saw my coworker's face. Her eyes were filled with concern but there was a gentle smile on her face, which was framed with plump curls. It calmed me further and I sat up. I allowed myself three deep breaths before speaking.

"What happened?" I asked.

"We were here in the bathroom talking. You were in distress because of the incident with the cop. And it triggered a panic attack for you."

I didn't know her very well, but she sounded so knowledgeable.

"I used to have panic attacks all the time," she said. "I get it. Just try to focus on your breath, and when you feel ready, we can get you up."

"The cop. What happened with the officer?" I said with panic in my voice—I was supposed to get the papers.

"We're handling that." She answered confidently. I believed her because she reported directly to the president of the company.

"I can't remember anything. I was walking across the parking lot to get my papers, and then I was here. How did I get in here with you?"

"Well, you came into the office and told Morgan the police were outside, and you needed proof of ownership. Morgan told you to stay behind and he went out with the paperwork. You looked calm but I saw your hands were shaking, so I brought you in here. You were splashing water on your face and telling me what happened and then you broke down. You must have been really terrified. I have a masters in therapy, but it doesn't take that to imagine how scared you were to have a cop pull a dog and a gun on you.

I still felt myself tremoring inside. I was still terrified. I wanted to go home. My girlfriend had my car. She dropped me off at work in the morning and then used my car to get around for job hunting.

I asked her to help me up. I straightened myself out and tested my legs for a few steps in place. I dared a glance in the mirror. My eyes were red, but I looked passable for facing my coworkers. At least Vivian was the only one who had witnessed my full freak out.

Morgan was returning from the front just as we exited the bathroom.

"Hey, I spoke with the officer. We're all good. He did say that the property line is basically so close to the property that we can never legally walk back there. The government has an easement on the rest of the property for security purposes. So next time we won't send you out there. The landscaper said he got what he needed, and he will call you with a quote."

Morgan was always a frank guy. He delivered and collected information concisely and effectively, but his affect was strange. From my perspective, the only emotion he seemed capable of was self-satisfaction. I liked that about him.

"Thank you for your help. That was all quite a shock for me." I looked in Vivian's direction. She gave an affirming nod.

"I can imagine. I saw that dog. I am terrified of dogs." Morgan said before walking away shaking his head at his own fears and caring little about mine. He was a Black engineer from another generation. I didn't blame or judge him for his social awkwardness.

I left work for the rest of the day and called in sick the next day to take a long weekend. I couldn't sleep at all the first night. The second I drifted off for a few minutes, I was locked in a state of terror for almost an hour. The roar. The sealed mouth and eyelids. The terrible, terrible gunfire, pounding to the beat of my heart. Once I was free from it, I refused to sleep after dark. Before this incident, the panic attacks had only happened during sleep at night. So, I stayed up all night long, waiting for the sky to turn blue enough to light my room to a level I felt safe to sleep in.

My girlfriend and I used this opportunity to have sex. Lots of sex. She was used to working overnight shifts. Though it seemed like forever since she had worked a job, she still kept night owl hours, watching TV and keeping watch for my nightmares, and the 24-hour terror that was Shine. I appreciated her for that, so I invested my newfound waking hours in her sexually. We took turns drowning in each other's sex for hours, giggling and laughing through teasing strokes between orgasms. Christine excited me in all the right ways. She was beautiful inside and out. I loved her imperfections because I was trying to embrace mine—which included a threat- slinging psycho ex-lover. What I appreciated most about Christine is that she liked me as much as I liked her.

While the state of my heart was strong, my brain was falling apart inside. Summer was in full force and that meant harder work at my job. I went to work exhausted each day from an intentionally sleepless night, watching the clock for my shift to end so I could race sunset home for a nap before nightfall. The few hours' sleep would have to last until after work the following day. Occasionally I would park my car in the far corner of the mostly vacant building garage and recline my seats for a nap. But I always felt it was too risky—after all, I was literally sleeping on the job.

After a week, I called my doctor. Then during my office visit with her I explained the attacks that were keeping me from sleeping at night.

She sighed as she handed over the starter pack of The Antidepressant.

"But this is an antidepressant. I'm not depressed," I said.

"Yes but it also treats anxiety, which you say you have. Take this at the same time every night. Schedule a follow up in four weeks and I will write you a prescription if it's helping you.

The pills felt heavy in my pocket as I carried them out of the office. At this stage I was so delirious from the lack of sleep and drained from the heat of summer, that I didn't care.

I set an alarm on my phone to go off at 11:00 p.m. every night. No matter what I was doing at that moment, when the alarm beeped, I popped The Antidepressant. I called it Crazy o' Clock when I was with my friends. I didn't have to call it anything with Christine. She knew what was happening.

I went back to sleeping at night on the second day of the pill. I didn't feel any different yet—my body just couldn't bear to endure the night awake anymore. I was reborn when I awoke the next morning. I gave the credit to the sleep, not The Antidepressant. Then I remembered the sleep might not have happened so peacefully without it. Which was like remembering that I was crazy.

I was obsessed with the thought of being on The Antidepressant. I didn't feel crazy—in fact I knew I wasn't. I have seen crazy—real crazy—hooting from every branch of my family tree. That wasn't me—not yet. Not so young.

I knew deep inside that I wasn't mentally ill. I was just afraid. I was afraid of Shine and what she would do, not to me or Christine or my property—but to herself. I couldn't handle the guilt if she actually hurt herself. I felt staying away was a way to protect myself and her. Clearly she was the one with the mental illness, and I was a trigger. I was terrified she would kill herself over me. The guilt would have consumed me. I resolved to keep her out of my life and stay out of hers. That way if the worst did ever happen, I wouldn't be there to experience it. I loved her, but I loved myself more. Now my fear of something bad happening with Shine was literally making me insane.

The Antidepressant turned down the fear long enough for me to get a good night sleep and not suffer more blackouts at work or anywhere else, so I was happy to be crazy for a few minutes a night.

Then, after two weeks on the medication, I woke up one morning and the world was all shades of gray and muted earth tones. Nothing popped with color, even the things I knew to be vibrantly colored, such as the trees, the sky, my Purple car, the sun, my skin. Everything might as well have all been the same color based on how it looked and felt to me. The world lost its beauty, even though it still looked completely the same.

I noticed the shift but didn't say anything about it. How do you explain that all of the colors are gone? I worried that my vision was going but I knew deep inside that it wasn't my eyes. It was the medication. I could tell that The Antidepressant was doing its job—slathering my brain in a coat of cope. Negotiating away color was a small price to pay to keep the fear at bay. At least that's what I told myself.

Sex died next. Well actually, it committed suicide. Lesbians don't need erections to have sex and so not having sex was largely a matter of choice over bodily function. But my body refused to choose to function sexually. It was as if someone had flipped a switch, and the same force that sucked the vibrant colors from the scenes of my life away also sent my libido swirling down the drain. Sex was physical color to me. Without its glorious hues, it was just flaps of multi-textured skin slapping and flicking at each other, sharing fluids, spreading bacteria. The thought repulsed me. I didn't even want to kiss Christine. The flavor of kissing was gone. When we did kiss, all I could think about were germs. Disgusting germs mixing into mucus soup in our mouths. The Antidepressant had cured one form of anxiety in me only to embolden another buried within—germaphobia.

Christine didn't complain about the lack of sex. I still wanted her there and close to me. She was unemployed and living with me rent-free. Even without sex, I was a great package. She needed me as much I needed her. She did comment on how The Antidepressant was affecting my personality.

"You could say it's erasing your personality," she said. "You used to laugh and smile and talk, but now you only have one emotion and it's...it's...I don't even know what to call it."

I couldn't argue with her. Arguing was color and color was gone. I merely noted her feedback and kept my 11:00 pm appointments with my crazy pills.

As summer dragged to an end I increasingly hated how I felt or, in truth, didn't feel. I felt *over-fixed*, like too much had been thrown at what was starting to feel like a small problem. Shine hadn't made contact in weeks. I missed happiness more than I missed nighttime sleep. Happiness was color. By then all of my emotions were a translucent shade of gray. All of my feeling was fading away.

Finally, I confided in Christine that she was right. My emotions were leaving me.

"They aren't leaving you." She said. "You're just chasing them away with that brain poison man."

I couldn't argue. She wasn't shaming me, it was truth. To kill fear in my brain I had to kill all emotion. The Antidepressant was like mental chemotherapy. It killed the good with the bad.

"I couldn't sleep. You were there. You saw what a wreck I was. I can't go back to that."

"Yeah I know babe." She said. I could see she understood my dilemma and wanted to help.

"Would you be open to trying some...alternative medication for what ails you?" She asked with carefully chosen words. I was a master at reading between the lines—a remnant of my days of sniffing out sin as an evangelist.

"Alternative medication as in?" I asked, knowing the answer but also knowing the implication of her honesty. I knew she smoked pot, but I abhorred drugs of any kind. I was especially averse to marijuana because I hated how dumb stoners became once they got high. During my months working at The Video Place and The Taco Place, I spent irrecoverable hours of my life trapped in pointless conversations with slow-moving potheads whose eyes were bloodshot and whose breath and bodies bore the skunk-like musk of weed. I had a strict rule when I moved into my own apartment—she was never to bring weed into my home. She also was not permitted to be noticeably stoned around me. No red eyes, no dumbass conversation, and no funky fragrance.

"Of the herbal variety..." she said slowly.

"Do you have some here?" I asked?

I tried to keep judgment from my tone, but my expression surely indicated that I wouldn't be pleased if the answer was yes.

"No." She answered. I was flooded with relief. She didn't break her promise.

"But," she continued, "I could."

"You could what?" I asked.

"Get some bud." She said plainly. "I have a friend. I can call him."

I was silent for a moment. One on hand, I instantly trusted her more for not having brought marijuana into my home like I asked. On the other hand, I had to admit a part of me was a little disappointed when she said no. I couldn't deny that dealing with anxiety by popping The Antidepressant every night had increased my compassion for people who chose to self-medicate with drugs and alcohol. Fear is painful, and The Antidepressant was known to dull pain. I had no idea what was in the little white pill I was taking, but I knew it didn't grow from the ground. Like marijuana did. I made my decision.

"Call him." I said, handing over my Metro PCS cell phone. She made a call, and she left shortly after, taking the keys to my car.

"Do you want to come with?" She said.

"No. I can't risk being caught."

She laughed a little and shrugged.

"Ok, I'll be back soon."

"Be careful baby," I said, feeling a twist in my stomach that I hadn't felt since I started taking The Antidepressant. I was afraid something bad would happen. I didn't know who this friend was. How guilty would I feel if she got caught...or worse.

Suddenly my brain remembered it was medicated and I felt myself calm down. Well, I didn't really calm down—it was more like I stopped caring. It was as if The Antidepressant had bullied my brain and forced it to hand those feelings over like lunch money, effectively starving my body of the emotion of concern.

Christine returned sooner than I expected her to. A part of me wondered if the deal had failed.

"Back so soon?"

"Yeah, she said. "I got lucky. He was in the area."

I had no idea getting drugs could be so easy, but I should have. I had seen members of my family somehow get drugs with ease, despite having nothing to offer and everything to lose.

Christine reached into her pocket and retrieved four small plastic pouches, each bulging with a nugget of green herb. She extended them to me in the palm of her hand. The smell hit me, and it wasn't as offensive as I remembered. However, fragrance was color, so my sense of smell and my reactions to scents was also diminished. I glanced down at them and finally plucked one of the pouches up between my finger and thumb, inspecting it closely.

"How much was this?" I asked.

"$5 each. They're called "nickel bags."

I rolled my eyes and snickered. "Thanks, I could put that much together."

"Well, I got four. So $20 worth. Should be good shit." She took a pouch with one hand and then put the other two back in her pocket. Then she opened the pouch, held it up to her nose and inhaled it deeply, sighing serenely. "It's blueberry."

"It's flavored weed?" I could feel my face crunch in confusion. I didn't know much about drugs, but I knew for sure that where I came from, weed didn't have flavors.

"That's the strain. There's different types. It's kinda like a flavor but it doesn't taste like blueberries. Unless you are really stoned, and you really want it to." She flashed me a loving smile.

She dipped her hands back into her pocket and retrieved something I recognized instantly—a small, yellow, rectangular package of TOP rolling papers. I had seen my father delicately pull many slivers of those papers from a package just like it nearly every summer, folding it over a shoebox lid as he sprinkled weed down the center line, and deftly twisted it from his fingers across his palms into a tiny joint. Then he'd slide the shoebox lid back under his bed, and head downstairs to the basement to play guitar. I smiled for a moment of rare nostalgia.

I wonder if Dad would support this decision?

Christine had now broken the nugget from her pouch into a small mound of herb on my kitchen counter. She reached into her bag and pulled out a small clear contraption covered in plastic.

"This is a joint roller." She explained. "I always carry it, and papers. Even if I don't have weed. Because you never know."

I admired her for a moment; she was so laid back. I really loved her for it. Even if she was about to lead me through the valley of drug temptation.

She picked the marijuana up in pinches and loaded it into the joint roller, setting it on top of the plastic sheath. She pressed it down tightly, locking a small part into place in the center. Then, she slid a sliver of rolling paper into the crease and rolled down on the outer edge slowly. I watched the roller suck the paper down and wrap it around the tube of tightly packed marijuana inside of it. When she reached the edge, she quickly licked along it. Then with two more rolls of her thumb, the paper disappeared completely into the roller. She unlocked the small part she had pressed into the center, and out popped the perfectly rolled joint, which she poured into her hand. She thrust it forward proudly.

"Whoa" was all I could manage. I looked at her like she had just performed black magic, my mouth agape.

"Yeah, it's a pretty cool trick. You can hand roll joints of course, but this makes them perfect every time." She said. I could sense she was really passionate about weed. I took a moment to appreciate that she had abstained from it for a long time while she stayed with me. I felt loved to know she had chosen me over something she clearly loved as well.

And now we are going to smoke it together.

I forced my mind to change the channel from the after-school specials blaring in my memory. DARE couldn't scare me straight or clean at this point. I needed to try this; I wanted to.

As if right on cue, my crazy alarm went off. It was 11:00 pm.

"Wait, let me take my pill first." I quickly retrieved one from the bathroom and swallowed it down. I wasn't worried about taking it with weed; the pills gave me no high feeling whatsoever. In fact, I was hoping the weed would help The Antidepressant. I didn't want to feel anxiety or fear, but goddamn it, I wanted to feel *something.*

"Let's go outside. I don't want to smoke in here." I said.

We stepped out into my patio balcony. It faced the parking lot and front gate so that we could see any cars leaving or departing. It was a quiet night in the complex, as usual. The apartment above me was still vacant, and I was in the corner unit, so I only shared one wall with another unit. He was a friendly Black guy who worked nights; I often saw him coming from work as I left. A silent parking lot, a vacant upstairs unit and a vacated unit next door, I knew there was no better place than there, and no better time than then to smoke weed. And no better person to do it with than Christine, who smiled warmly at me still. The yellow streetlights cast shadows across her puffy cheeks and made the rippled ringlets of her long curly hair shimmer. I tried to smile back but I guess I looked afraid in the dark to her.

"Don't worry baby," she reassured me. "Nothing bad will happen."

She lifted the joint to her lips and lit it with a green lighter. She took a long drag before carrying the joint away from her mouth between the tips of her index finger and thumb. She placed it before her face, holding her breath for a few seconds before exhaling the smoke onto its burning tip, causing it to crackle and glow a bright red.

"Oh, that's hitting real nice," She said. Then she reached over and passed it to me.

I took it the same way she was holding it, pinching it between my right index finger and thumb. I chuckled a bit as I realized my hand was forming the sign for "OK" in American Sign Language.

"Okay, here goes nothing." I placed the joint between my lips, and took a teeny, tiny breath. It was barely enough to taste smoke in my mouth. As soon as I inhaled, I exhaled, as if I wanted to spit the smoke out.

I looked up with guilt at Christine as I passed the joint back, sure I hadn't done it right.

"You'll get the hang of it." She said, taking the joint and sucking from it again. She paused without exhaling, then hit it again. A broad grin spread across her face as she exhaled and was bathed in a cloud of smoke.

"Puff puff pass my love. That's the rotation. Puff puff pass."

The joint came back to me, and I tried to hit it properly, taking two small sucks from the now moist tip on the joint's unlit end. However, some kind of gag reflex was preventing me from inhaling the smoke into my lungs. I could only suck it into my mouth, and then immediately blow it back out. My mind flashed to President Bill Clinton and his famous quote that he had tried marijuana but "didn't inhale it." This made me giggle out loud a little bit. The sound of my own laughter surprised me. I passed the joint back to Christine.

Am I feeling it? I wondered. Searching myself for a different feeling. There was none.

Christine, on the other hand, was clearly getting high.

"Ohhh my sweet sweet herb. It's been sooo long." she sang softly to the joint, hitting it again.

I glanced down at my watch—we had been outside smoking for about 10 minutes, and I felt nothing. Nothing but disappointment. I wanted to cry.

Christine tried to pass the joint back to me, but I refused it.

"Nah, you go ahead babe. I'm good."

She didn't push. For a moment I wondered if it was because she was glad to have the rest to herself.

"Let her have her fun." I thought. "At least she tried to help."

I went inside and crawled into bed, still feeling absolutely nothing, even though I could smell weed everywhere.

The next day was Friday. As my workday dragged on uneventfully. I reflected on my weed-ventures from the previous night.

What a rip. I thought. I sucked on that thing at least three times and I didn't feel anything at all. Maybe there was something wrong with the weed?

Then I thought of how gleeful and chill Christine had seemed on the patio after just a couple of hits. She definitely felt it.

"I must be too crazy to get high." I thought.

With a jolt, I snapped out of it.

No! I said to myself, forcefully. *I'm not* too crazy to do anything. I'm *not* crazy.

So, I decided that I would try to smoke again. We had a three-day weekend ahead. Labor Day. I also happened to be sharing my 24th birthday with the holiday. We still had weed left. I figured Christine knew better than to smoke it while I was at work.

On my way home from work that night I stopped at the liquor store and splurged on a bottle of my favorite tequila—a tall, cobalt blue bottle of Correlejo Reposado. It was a splurge at $30, but I didn't care. It was my birthday. It was a holiday weekend. And it was payday.

"Fuck it." I said out loud. "If I can't get high, I can at least get drunk."

When I walked in the house, Christine greeted me warmly as she always did, planting a kiss on my lips.

"Happy birthday baby." She had made dinner of baked chicken and, my favorite, fried plantains.

I held up the bottle of tequila. "It's Friday night. Ain't shit to do. Might as well..."

She joined in to finish the phrase with me:

"...get fucked up Boo."

We both laughed. I took the tequila into the kitchen, washed my hands, and began to fix us dinner plates. Christine spread a blanket out on the living room floor. I didn't have furniture, except a desk and office chair where my computer and printer were set up. Shine's mother had bought all the furniture in our previous apartment, so of course her family took it all when they came to get her. All I owned was my bed, my computer and desk, a small TV, and the digital piano Shine bought me for my birthday. I didn't mind the empty space. It made me feel like my apartment was always clean. Christine and I loved to spread out on the floor and play cards. We could occasionally raise a TV program on my static-ey small color TV; neither of us were into television much. We both preferred to let the internet entertain us.

Soon we were seated cross-legged on the blanket together, chomping on juicy chicken and biting into crispy, salty slices of plantains.

"Mmmm thank you for making my favorite baby. Everything is delicious."

"You're welcome my love."

When we were done eating, Christine cleared the dishes while I prepped tequila shots. I sliced a lime that was on its last legs but still had enough juice to sooth the bite of a tequila shot.

My home was short of several basic kitchen essentials, but I did have a set of shot glasses that I bought on clearance at the Marshall's. I placed the saltshaker in the center of a dinner plate and put a shot glass on both sides of it. Then I surrounded them with my petrified lime slices. I picked the plate up in one hand and the bottle of Correlejo in the other, joining Christine again on the emptied blanket in the living room.

I poured two shots, and we downed them. I figured it was time to let the fun begin, if any fun could be wrung out of my SSRI-soaked brain. I loved Correlejo because it felt light and smooth going down my throat—not bitter and rough like José. I didn't even need salt. I sucked on the wedge of lime, relieving it of its last morsel of juice to chase the tequila, which was already settling in my full stomach.

"I have a present for you," Christine said with a smile.

"I like presents," I answered. It was true, but after my experience with Shine and I lavishing gifts on each other, I was quite comfortable with not having any pressure to spend money on each other. All my money went to having a roof over our heads, having my car on the road, and putting food in my belly.

I didn't see that my financial support of Christine was a great gift, although I know it was. It often did bother me that she didn't have a job and didn't seem to be urgently looking for one. But on the other hand, I had asked her to be there. I hadn't asked her to contribute financially because I knew she wouldn't. She didn't have to stay with me. She had free housing at home, so she wasn't going to pay to live in mine. And I didn't need her to pay me as much as I needed her to be there with me. Which she was, right then, on my birthday. With a gift for me.

"Well, where is it?" I asked in a sarcastically bossy tone.

Christine reached into the left side pocket of the jeans she wore every single day and pulled out a small package wrapped in bubble wrap, sealed with a rubber band, and set it on our living room picnic blanket.

I picked it up and noticed it was hard, but light. Something made of glass, which explained the bubble wrap. I peeled off the rubber band and unrolled the item from its protective casing. It was a small cobalt blue glass piece. It looked suggestive, sitting in my palm like a curvaceous woman with tits and hips.

"Ummm...what is it? A dildo?" I asked.

Christine burst out laughing as she poured us another round of tequila shots.

"No babe."

I laughed with her. It was too small to be a dildo. Clearly the tequila was kicking in. I gulped my third shot down, skipping lime this time.

I held the gift up to my face and inspected it closely. This womanly glass object had a face that sank into a small hollow centered at the top of her head, and a small hole on the side of it. There was another small hole at the bottom of her feet.

"It's a pipe," Christine explained. "You pack that bowl right there," she said, pointing to the tiny crater at the top. "cover the carb on the side, light it, and hit that shit."

She was incredibly proud to be sharing this information with me. That raised my suspicions a bit.

Bowl. I remember her playing some songs that mentioned smoking "bowls." I never knew what it meant, as all weed smokers in my family smoked joints around me. The only drug I knew to be smoked out of a glass pipe was crack.

"You got me a crack pipe for my birthday?" The words sounded ridiculous tumbling from my mouth. That tended to happen on tequila. Four shots were my maximum tolerance and I was already on three. On three shots of tequila, a crack pipe was a plausible gift from my white girlfriend.

"No babe," she hooted. "You use it to smoke weed."

"Oh, really?" I said, now allowing myself to feel a little excitement about the gift. I finally found my gratitude.

"Thank you." I said with a smile. "So, are we going to smoke out of it?"

"Hell yeah," she exclaimed. "It's your birthday."

She reached into her right jeans pocket and retrieved a packet of weed.

Nickel bag. I let loose a giggle.

I was feeling loose and ready to try weed again. I decided we should stay inside this time. I didn't care about the smell.

Christine opened the baggie and pinched a bud out, then crumbled it into the bowl, which was still in my hand.

"Pack that in," she said.

I pushed on the crumbled marijuana gently, packing it into the bowl.

"Ok, the trick to this is you have to cover the hole on the side while you light it. That's the carb. You start inhaling so smoke fills the chamber of the pipe. Then you release the carb, inhale all the smoke into your lungs and blow it out."

That seemed like a lot of steps. I wasn't crazy about having fire that close to my face. I also couldn't unsee the images of shivering crackheads I'd seen in movies, huddled in corners using lighters to blaze addictive smoke into their lungs.

I stared at the bowl. The weed in it looked innocent and earthy. It didn't look like crack. It wasn't crack. It was marijuana. I shoved my flame fears aside.

"Pass me the lighter," I told Christine. She retrieved a Bic lighter from her pocket.

"Damn, those jeans are ready for everything," I said.

Following Christine's instructions, I cupped the pipe in my left hand, plugging the side hole with my thumb, lit the lighter and lowered it into the weed as I slowly inhaled through the bottom hole. The chamber filled with smoke as she said, and I could taste the weed in my mouth. I lifted my thumb away from the carb, and inhaled a deep breath, sucking all of the smoke in.

"Hold it for a few seconds if you can," she said.

I somehow managed to hold it in. There was a short pause before my lungs exploded into a cough. I coughed and barked and choked and yet it seemed impossible to empty my lungs of all the smoke I inhaled. I could see it still rushing out of my mouth and nose. I kept coughing. The sound of my own coughing rang in my ears like thunderous booms. It seemed that the smoke had evaporated all of saliva from my mouth and throat. As I continued to gasp and sputter, I started to struggle to breathe. The smoke I was exhaling seemed to fill the room.

Smoke was filling the room. Smoke? Where did all this smoke come from?

My vision was blurry, and I suddenly couldn't see Christine at all. All I could see was clouds of smoke surrounding her and suffocating me. The smoke was suffocating me. No, the smoke was coming from me. Suddenly I was outside of my own body, and I could see myself, coughing and smoking. I was on fire. My head was on fire.

I jumped up from the floor and started running in a panic around the living room.

"Help. I'm on fire. Help me." I barely heard the sound of Christine's voice, muffled by the thick smoke and my cacophony of hysteria. I rushed towards the patio door, but as I reached it I saw blaring lights streaming in from outside.

"Oh no it's the police. I need the fire department. Not the police."

"Calm down babe. Calm down."

The room was moving and swirling as I ran around it, fanning at my own head, which I was sure was burning, somehow painlessly, from my throat up. I felt a hand grab my arm firmly and wrestle me down a sitting position. I continued to shriek, certain that my life was ending. Something about Christine's touch was comforting at that moment as I leaned into it.

"Here. Drink this," she said lifting a cup to my lips. I took a small sip and felt an immediate cooling sensation in my mouth and throat. My next sips were fast and deep. As I swallowed them, emptying the glass, I noticed that the smoke was gone too. The cool, clear water had quenched the drunken, fiery hallucination that had been triggered by cottonmouth, courtesy of my first bowl hit of blueberry kush. My mouth and throat were back to normal, but my state of mind was still very altered. This was it.

"I'm high." I said. "And I'm drunk. I'm drunk and I'm high."

Christine would end up quoting me on this frequently in the months that followed, but at that moment she withheld teasing.

"Let's play some music." she said.

Christine went to the computer and opened my music player, which was generously filled with a library of music I had downloaded for free. She clicked a selection and the sounds of Floetry filled the apartment. The sound of the music struck a deep joy in me. It had been a while since I had felt this way hearing music. On The Antidepressant, music hadn't moved me as much. I started to sway a little and my heart rate finally normalized from my earlier state of terror.

"Hey, come look at this," she said, inviting me to get up and have a seat in the sole piece of furniture in my house—my desk chair.

I took a seat, and she clicked the button to take my computer's media player into full screen mode. It began to display a blissful array of morphing fractal shapes. I felt overwhelming joy as I watched them.

"These visualizations are groovy when you're buzzed. Just watch, listen to the music, relax and vibe. You're home and you're safe, babe," Christine said.

I peered at the computer screen, watching the shapes expand and collapse, float up and drop back down, twist and loop in time with Floetry's neosoul rhythms, all while cycling through the rainbow of colors. Colors. Beautiful colors. I could see them. Red. Orange. Yellow. Green. Blue. Purple. I even saw cyan and maroon. I could see color again.

I stared at my computer like I was looking into my own soul. I don't know how long I stayed there like that, but when I finally looked away, several songs deep into the album, I knew that I had found myself again. Yes, I'd had a long bad trip, but the journey had ultimately landed me right where I wanted to be. Able to experience joy. Able to see color. Able to feel music. All of that from one hit of weed.

When was the last time I felt truly happy?

I sat in silence with the thought. Then my mind travelled back three years and three thousand miles to California. My mental time machine returned me to the shores of glorious Southern California beaches where I had once lain on the rocks with the sun in my face as the waves roared towards me.

That is where I am meant to be.

At that very moment, I knew.

I'm going back to California.

One pivotal moment in my move was when I crossed the GA state line into Alabama, I chucked the last of The Antidepressant out the window of my car. It took me over a year to find the courage to try medicinal marijuana when I got out to California, but once I did, I never looked back.

###

CARPE THE DIEM

By March 2004, I was settled and content in Los Angeles. I landed a good job at a start-up charter school. I had my own apartment Los Angeles' Koreatown with a view of the Hollywood sign. The world seemed mine for the taking. When I looked across my life, the only thing I could truly ask for was more friends to fill my idle time.

I broke up with Christine four months after I arrived in California. She was supposed to join me. I asked her raise $1000 to contribute to our living expenses during the trip and the move. She wasn't able to find the money. Meanwhile, I sold everything I owned to fund the trip. I was sad to leave Christine behind. I loved her and would miss her. Like a true Sagittarius, she was about where she was. Meanwhile, like a Virgo, I was about where I was going. So, I broke up with her via instant messenger. She wasn't surprised.

"Long distance relationship never work," she said with sadness in her voice.

"But, maybe a long distance friendship will?" I offered, hoping to console her.

"We'll see," she said.

It was the last time we ever contacted each other.

I was both relieved by the breakup, and restless from it. I'm the type of person who loves to accomplish two things at once. One evening I was standing in my apartment, smoking a bowl at my window. After I blew out an exceptionally large hit, I wondered out loud what would be the best way to keep busy and make more friends.

Suddenly, a burst of inspiration hit me. What if I got a part-time job? Something that would make extra money and make new friends. There was only one place I could imagine wanting to work that could fulfill both aims. I went to my computer and did a quick search for the nearest video rental store.

Just my luck, there was a store two miles away from my apartment that was hiring new team members. I quickly completed an online application, attaching my resume and a custom letter describing my positive experiences as a previous employee of the chain.

The following morning, I got a call from Roger, the manager of that local store, asking me to stop by for an interview that evening. I showed up for my interview still dressed in business casual clothing from my day job. Roger puffed on a cigarette and looked me up and down a couple of times before he began my interview while we stood on the steps just outside of the store.

"Well, you certainly dressed to impress," he said.

"It is a job interview," I replied. "I would have worn my old uniform, but it didn't make the trip to California with me."

Roger took a long drag of his cigarette and exhaled it to the side. "I read your cover letter. Very impressive. Do you know how many job applications I've received with a cover letter in all of my years working for this company."

"No sir, I do not."

"None. Zero. Yours was the first cover letter. And it was good too."

I shuffled awkwardly, looking down at him as he smoked and pondered aloud about my level of professionalism. *Am I going to get this job?*

"I had to meet this person who wrote such a passionate cover letter for a job at a video rental store that pays minimum wage," he continued.

I waited for him to ask me a question.

"You're overqualified for this position," he said. "Why do you want to work here?"

"Honestly, I'm just looking to make money and friends. I have a Monday through Friday nine to five, but I need something to fill the six to midnights and the weekends. In college, this is what I did. So, I figured, why not do it again? Plus, I live right down the street."

Roger extinguished his cigarette by smashing it into the handrail of the stairs.

"See the thing about this job is you can't hire people who are too smart. Smart people don't stay. Case in point, myself, who has worked for this company for going on 13 years. I'm not smart. But you are. So, why should I hire you?"

I thought for a second, and then gave the only logical answer I knew.

"Because I can do the job and I want to."

Roger reached into his pocket, pulled out another cigarette and lit it. I felt sweat forming in the armpits of my blouse.

"Like I said, the job pays minimum wage. That's $6.75 an hour to start."

"I have 2 years of experience at this job and open availability to close nights and weekends. I'll accept $7.25 to start," I countered.

He exhaled his puff of smoke with a laugh. "See? This is why you can't hire people who are too smart. I can't start you at $7.25, even though I'm sure you're worth every penny."

"Then hire me," I said, feeling very smart as I stared at him in sweaty business casual clothes.

"$7 an hour. Be here tomorrow at 6pm," he said.

I reached out and shook his hand. "Thank you. I'll see you tomorrow."

"Oh, and…," he continued, "don't wear that. Jeans are fine."

"Heard that," I replied.

Things worked out very well for me at the video store. I was content with my new routine. I worked at the charter school from 8:00 a.m. to 5:00 p.m. Monday through Friday. Fridays and Saturday evenings, I closed at the video store. Sundays were my day off. I usually spent Sundays watching videos and surfing the internet, smoking weed when I had some, and getting drunk off of $2 wine I stocked up when I did my weekly grocery shopping. All I wanted was more of a social life. And a car–the engine on the purple Ford that had escorted me to California had died. My car sat in the shop waiting for me to raise the $3000 required to fix it. Meanwhile, I took public transportation or taxis everywhere. Luckily, both commutes were easy. I lived and worked near Metro station stops to get to my day job. The video store was a two-mile bus ride up Wilshire Blvd, with stops one block away from my apartment and the store. The bus ran every 15-20 minutes until 1:30 a.m.

The video store kept me around people but it wasn't the best place to make friends. My coworkers were all much younger than I. None of them were Black. None of them were queer. The store's customers weren't my kind of people either. They were mostly drunks and stoners, stumbling in to purchase cheap entertainment and munchies with what was left of their disposable incomes. Otherwise, we got overwhelmed parents looking for a distraction for their gaggles of sticky-fingered children. Both groups could disarrange all the freshly organized rows of videotape covers in mere seconds. Even though I wasn't making friends, I was making enough extra money to buy weed, keep my nails manicured, and go for the occasional happy hour with the few friends I had.

Every now and then, Roger would ask me to pick up a shift that wasn't on my schedule. I said yes whenever I could. When he called me one Sunday afternoon to ask if I could come work four hours that evening, I agreed, as long as I didn't have to close.

"I only need you to work the rush, so come at 6 and leave at 10. I have a new gal starting and I don't think she's ready to handle the rush alone, but I got no one else that can go train her. I'll come in at 8 to close."

When I strolled into the store at 5:45, it was packed with customers. I saw my coworker, Marina, working diligently behind one cashwrap, with a line that stretched to the back of the store. Marina was the best employee in the store. Her sales numbers were untouchable, and she was great with the customers.

"Open over there and help me clear this line. I gotta go pick up my kids," Marina said.

I quickly complied.

Behind the other cashwrap, I saw the new girl, who was checking in returned videos and DVDs from an overflowing bin. I clocked in, opened and counted a new till, and called for the next customer. Within 20 minutes, the line was cleared, and Marina was clocked out. I turned to check the progress on the return bin. It was empty, but there were still many movies needing to be reshelved.

"I can help you out with this until the next customer comes in," I offered to the girl. "I'm KishaLynn."

"I'm Donna," she said and flashed a big smile that matched the recognizable Southern hospitality in her voice. Donna was short in stature and white in color. Her skin was a very pale white, which made her blue gray eyes stand out, as did her rosy cheeks. Her teeth were white and perfectly straight. Her hair was also white–not blonde, not gray–but white. I had never seen a white woman who was whiter than Donna. I wondered if she was an albino but knew it would be rude to ask.

Something stirred within me when I shook Donna's hand. I immediately noticed that she was older than I was, which was refreshing. I got the feeling that she was also a lesbian. She just had a rainbow vibe that went along with her alabaster complexion. Together, we quickly returned all the movie cases to their shelves. Then, I opened a register for Donna next to mine, and began to train her on how to check out customers, since Marina had been too busy to do so earlier.

Roger strolled in right at 8pm as promised, just as the final rush of the evening was beginning. He was impressed that I had Donna going on the registers. With three lines open, the Sunday night rush went smoothly.

At 10 pm, Roger told me I could clock out to go. "Donna, you can also clock out. I'll close up on my own."

"Are you sure you don't need help, Roger?" I asked.

"Nah. Been doing this for years. I've got it covered. Thanks."

"Cool," I said. "Next bus comes in 10 minutes. I'll see you Friday. Donna, it was nice meeting you."

"Hey, you don't have to catch the bus. I drove my truck today. Let me give you a ride."

"Even better," I said, secretly celebrating the blessing of making a new friend with a vehicle.

The moment I climbed into the passenger seat in Donna's truck, she opened the ashtray under the radio, pulled out a joint and lit it.

Oh, hell yes. I thought, thanking God again for a new friend who shared my favorite vice.

"I live at 5th and Catalina," I said. Then I took a huge hit from Donna's joint as she turned left on Wilshire Boulevard and began the drive towards my apartment in Koreatown.

"So, where did you come from and where the hell have you been?" I asked. Then I rolled down her passenger window to exhale my hit into the night air.

Donna laughed at my questions. "Well, I come from Texas. And now I'm here, and I've been here?"

"You just started here?"

"Yeah, I was bored and needed something to do."

I was amazed. "That's exactly why I started working here too. I moved here alone almost a year ago. In fact, my LA anniversary is coming up. I'm not big on the party scene, but I worked at this store in college, so I figured it would be a good way to make friends. And now, here you are."

The weed and the glee were both getting to me. For a moment I feared I was being weird.

"So, what brought you out here from Texas?"

"What else?" she answered, "A girl."

"Oh yeah? Cool. How's that working out?"

"It didn't," she replied.

"Oh. Sorry to hear that."

Donna hit her joint twice and then passed it back to me. "That's life," she responded on her exhale.

"When's your next shift?" I asked.

"I don't know. I'm not sure if I'll go back."

"What? You're quitting? You just started."

"Ha, I know. I worked there long enough." I thought about Roger telling me about hiring smart people. Donna was definitely smart.

"Oh man, but I just met you," I whined.

"You're funny," Donna said with a laugh. "But here's the thing–you *met* me. You know me now, even if we don't work together."

She was very practical, and I loved it about her right away.

"That's true," I said.

"I wish I could say I'm not going anywhere, but…I'm headed back to Texas. It's too expensive out here," Donna continued.

I felt like crying. So much for a new friend. I was surprised at how quickly I had become invested in Donna. I had just met her five hours ago, and I had cycled through the full spectrum of emotion on the two-mile ride down Wilshire Boulevard.

"This is my turn right here. Pull up in front of The DuBarry," I said, trying to hide the disappointment in my voice.

"Aww, what's wrong sweetheart?" Donna said. Her Southern drawl wrapped me like a blanket of authentic concern as she parked in the loading zone in front of my apartment building and killed the engine.

"Sorry, I'm high. And also, I was excited to make a friend. Pull over right here."

"Wow, what's with all the past tense? And why be so dramatic? You were looking for a friend. You made one. I'm right here." Donna gave me a wave. "I gave you a ride home and we smoked a joint. It's a great night."

I couldn't help but laugh.

"All very true," I said. "I have a tendency to get emotional, especially when I'm high."

"You don't have to explain yourself. I'm just advising you to enjoy the moment. You manifested it. Hey, have you ever seen the movie *The Secret?"*

"No. What's that?"

"It's a movie about the law of attraction. You should check it out. Then you'll know what I mean when I say you manifested this."

I stared at Donna, certain now that she was as stoned as I. However, a feeling tingling in my gut told me that none of this was a coincidence. Something felt destined about the moment. I made a mental note to check out *The Secret.*

"Well, since we don't work together anymore," I said lightheartedly, "Maybe we can hang out soon–before you go? I'm thinking about having a party to celebrate my LA anniversary next week. Let's exchange numbers."

"Absolutely," Donna said. We exchanged numbers and then I waved goodbye to Donna.

As I lay in bed that night, I recapped the evening, thinking about what Donna had said about manifesting.

What a strange white girl. I'll probably never hear from her again.

******

One week after I celebrated my one-year anniversary in Los Angeles, I was getting off the Red Line escalator at the Wilshire/Vermont Station coming home from work on a Friday, my phone rang, which it almost never did. Miraculously, I answered it, which I almost never do.

It was Donna calling. I had last seen her at my anniversary party, where she had delivered a rousing and X-rated rendition of Pat Benatar's *Hit Me With Your Best Shot.*

"GirlBar tonight?" she asked.

"Nah...not really feeling it," I replied. "I'm still recovering from my anniversary party hangover from last weekend. I want to lay low and veg out."

"Come on. It's one of my last Fridays before I move back to Texas. How about just having early cocktails? It's happy hour–two drinks for one–at Ultrasuede starting at 4:00 p.m. We don't have to stay out late. And I'll come get you."

"Sold," I told her, "But I'm not dressing up."

"Deal. You always look gorgeous anyway," Donna said.

I really didn't dress up. In fact, when I met Donna outside, I was still dressed in my work casual Friday garb of faded black jeans, a black lace top with a hole in the arm, and tennis shoes. My hair was carelessly slung back in a ponytail. I didn't wear makeup, not even lip gloss.

We were the first people in the door at Club Ultrasuede in West Hollywood that night. I had never been there so early. It was just as well because I wasn't doing the typical night out. I did feel self-conscious about how underdressed I was, so when we picked the table right by the door, I made sure that my back was facing the entrance as Donna and I started in on our cocktails.

A few hours later, the place was starting to look more GirlBar. I was feeling my double raspberry kamikaze cocktails on the rocks. Donna and I were chatting it up, discussing life and love. I hadn't known her for long, but her worldview fascinated me. She was so positive and real. It made me emotional.

"Thank you," I yelled to Donna across the table. "I'm glad I came out. I'm having a great time."

"Oh my God, you're such a sap," Donna teased back at me.

Suddenly I got the urge to turn around and look at the entrance behind me. Just as I did, the door curtains parted, and a woman stepped in.

A tall, brown, *sexy* woman with short platinum blond hair. I did a double take as she walked past me.

"Damn," I told Donna. "Never seen her here before."

"Who?"

Donna had somehow managed to miss her, so I stood in my seat conspicuously scanning the room for her again to point her out. I was six cocktails in, so all subtlety was lost. I spotted the girl by the bar.

"Good Lord, she is fine as hell. And Black. And tall. And a Girl. At GirlBar. God knows this place is usually filled with women who are none of the above."

Donna was laughing at me by then because I was so incredibly pressed.

"Here's an idea," she said, "Go talk to her."

I looked at her like she was crazy.

"Never," I said. "Do you see what I have on? Do you see my hair? I am not about to try and holler at a girl looking like this. Besides, I'm off the game. I had one bad date too many."

With that, I sat back down and started to sip my drink again. That's when Donna reached across the table and snatched it from me.

"Goodbye," she said.

"What?"

"I'm holding your drink hostage. Now, go away, and don't come back without that girl, or her number."

Fuck. I had that tingly feeling in my gut again that told me I had to listen to Donna. There was no point in protesting. I had plenty of liquid courage running through my veins. The girl was standing by the bar next to the restroom.

What the hell? I thought. *If I'm rejected, at least I can also go take a piss.*

So, off I went. I walked across the almost empty dance floor, headed straight towards her easy-to-spot platinum hair.

Just as I got within earshot of her, I lost my nerve and bluffed past her, jumping in the line for the bathroom instead.

The bathroom line was long. I felt like an idiot for punking out.

Come on KishaLynn. All you have to do is say hello. Do it. *If you don't, what will you tell Donna? Time to carpe the diem.*

So, I swung around and took a deep breath, smoothing my hair back in its ponytail. I walked to the bar and approached the tall, brown, sexy woman.

"Excuse me...hi. My name is Lynn...what's yours?"

"I'm Shelli...with an I." The next thing I heard was BOW! as the DJ's speakers began to bump a favorite song of mine-Shake by the Ying Yang Twins. I couldn't resist.

"Shelli, with an I, would you like to dance?"

She said yes and off we went to the dance floor, which had many more people on it because of the popular song. We danced the entire song. I completely forgot about how I was dressed. I completely forgot about my hair. All I cared about was the music, and the girl. I danced my ass off. The song was winding down, and I thought our dance was too, but then, the fates aligned and...Beyonce!

As Check On It started to pour through the speakers next, she kept dancing, so I did too. It was Beyonce after all. Once I could tell that this Shelli "With An I" loved the song, and Beyonce, as much as I did, I pulled her close, tucking my fingertips under her belt and danced my heart into this girl.

When the song ended, I remembered Donna's challenge. I invited Shelli "With an I" back to our table and introduced her to Donna. Donna high-fived me for rising to the challenge and coming back with the girl *and* the number.

"I know you're not from around here. Where are you from?" I asked Shelli.

"I moved here from Phoenix," she said. "But I'm originally from Columbus."

"Tell me you mean Columbus, Georgia?" I asked.

"No. Columbus, Ohio."

It felt like my heart stopped.

"No fucking way," I said, way too loudly. "I'm from Columbus. Wow, that's a first. I've never met a girl from home before. What do you do?"

"I'm actually a chef," she replied.

That restarted my heart, which from that moment began to beat only for her. I had felt, from the moment I had laid eyes on Shelli "With An I," *This one's mine.*

THE END…FOR NOW…

EPILOGUE: BROWNSEXY

crystals melting
into liquid platinum
brownsexy
makes me feel
like sweet
turning into
spicy
couldn't know joy better
smile she carries
big as her love
brownsexy
rule the world
be mine
you
are
so
beautiful
.
every beat of
my heart
calls her
brownsexy

###

ABOUT THE AUTHOR

KishaLynn Moore Elliott is a Black lesbian artist and healer. She is the author of A D.R.E.A.M. Comes True: Five Steps to Planning and Creating Your Personal Success Story NOW, and CHILDish: Stories From the Life of a Young Black Girl. BLACK WOMAN GROWN is her latest collection of personal stories about growing up too soon, turning tragedies into triumphs along the way. She currently lives in San Diego with her wife and son. She graduated from Spelman College in 2002.